DENVER, COLORADO

Top Of The Town Directory .com

Kitchen Distributors Inc
1309 West Littleton Boulevard
Littleton, CO 80120
(303) 795-0665
info@kitchendistributors.com
www.kitchendistributors.com

e3 Design Group, Inc.
12150 West 44th Avenue
Wheat Ridge, CO 80033
(303) 908-9770
jimmy@e3designgroupinc.com
www.e3designgroupinc.com

In-Site Design Group Inc.
1280 South Clayton Street
Denver, CO 80210
(303) 691-9000
insite@insite-design-group.com
www.insite-design-group.com

Closet Factory
8480 Upland Drive, Suite 200
Centennial, CO 80112
(303) 690-6901
mark.lestikow@closetfactory-colorado.com
www.denver.closetfactory.com

closet factory

Geist Flooring
475 West 115th Avenue, Suite 2
Northglenn, CO 80234
(303) 919-4604
geistflooring@yahoo.com
www.geistflooring.com

TreeLine Homes, Inc
1727 Fifteenth Street, Suite 200
Boulder, CO 80302
(303) 449-2371
derek@treelineboulder.com
www.treelinehomes.com

Top of the Town Directory

DENVER, COLORADO

Top of the Town Directory is an exclusive

collection of elite professionals-professionals

recommended as the best-of-the-best by their

clients and peers alike. Selected for their

outstanding craftsmanship and unbeatable

service, these professionals have a reputation

for setting the bar in their respective trades;

for delivering exceptional quality in every

detail of every job.

Acupuncturist

Uptown Acupuncture
549 East 19th Avenue
Denver, CO 80203
(303) 200-0491
michael.lay@comcast.net

Appliances

DC&A Cabinets & Appliances
5969 North Broadway
Denver, CO 80216
(303) 292-9830
cindy.h@kitchensofcolorado.com
discountcabinets.com

Architect

Virginia DuBrucq, AIA, LLC
1919 East Mississippi Avenue
Denver, CO 80209
(303) 698-2200
ginnydubrucq@qwestoffice.net

Art Gallery

Art Source and Design
Available Thru Your Interior Designer
1111 West Evans Avenue, Suite C
Denver, CO 80223
(303) 936-4212
asdesign@artsource-design.com
www.artsource-design.com

Awnings and Patio Coverings

SunSaver Retractable Awnings, Inc.
5978 South Nome Street
Englewood, CO 80111
(303) 694-6847
shademe@sunsaverawnings.com
www.sunsaverawnings.com

Banker

Citywide Banks
Deb Neeley, Vice President
10660 East Colfax Avenue
Aurora, CO 80010
(303) 365-3658
neeley@citywidebanks.com
www.citywidebanks.com

Cabinetry

Connolly Custom Cabinets
(970) 490-27815432
john@connollycabinets.com
connollycabinets.com

Closets and Storage

Closet Factory
8480 Upland Drive, Suite 200
Centennial, CO 80112
(303) 690-6901
mark.lestikow@closetfactory-colorado.com
www.denver.closetfactory.com

Drywall and Plaster

Drywall Systems
Ben Borrego
(303) 349-3650
bborrego@mesanetworks.net

Electricians

Weimer Electric
12150 West 44th Avenue, Suite 111
Wheat Ridge, CO 80033
(303) 422-7428
joe@weimerelectricinc.com
www.weimerelectricinc.com

Flooring

Coventry Carpet & Flooring
2618 West Barberry Place
Denver, CO 80204
(303) 768-8599
scot@coventrycarpets.com
www.coventrycarpets.com

Framing, Art

Frame de Art
3065 South Broadway
Englewood, CO 80113
(303) 722-1525
framedeart@aol.com

Top
Of
The
Town
Directory
.com

BOA Construction Inc.
Home Builder and Remodeling Contractor

Closet Factory
Closets and Storage

Comstock Design, LLC
Interior Designer

Hardwoods & Flooring Installer

Geist Flooring
475 West 115th Avenue, Suite 2
Northglenn, CO 80234
(303) 919-4604
geistflooring@yahoo.com
www.geistflooring.com

Home Accents

Elements for Design
Available Thru Your Interior Designer
1111 West Evans Avenue, Suite C-1
Denver, CO 80223
(303) 934-2465
kevin@elementsfordesign.net
www.elementsfordesign.net

Home Automation

Digital Media Innovations
3065 South Broadway
Englewood, CO 80113
(303) 873-1100
greg@digitalmediainnovations.com
www.digitalmediainnovations.com

e3 Design Group, Inc.
12150 West 44th Avenue
Wheat Ridge, CO 80033
(303) 908-9770
jimmy@e3designgroupinc.com
www.e3designgroupinc.com

Home Builder and Remodeling Contractor

BOA Construction Inc.
1339 Osage Street
Denver, CO 80204
(303) 892-1973
info@boaaaa.com
www.boaaaa.com

Fuller Custom Home & Remodel
8400 East Crescent Parkway, Suite 600
Greenwood Villiage, CO 80111
(303) 601-9446
gary@fullercustomhome.com
www.fullercustomhome.com

TreeLine Homes, Inc
1727 Fifteenth Street, Suite 200
Boulder, CO 80302
(303) 449-2371
derek@treelineboulder.com
www.treelinehomes.com

Home Improvement Education

NHIENetwork
PO Box 147
Sedalia, CO 80135
(720) 641-1864
ben@nhienetwork.com
www.nhienetwork.com

Interior Designer

Amirob Architectural Interior Designers
1948 Blake Street
Denver, CO 80202
(303) 296-7388
info@amirob.com
www.amirob.com

Comstock Design, LLC
5559 South Washington Street
Littleton, CO 80121
(303) 761-2440
gc@comstockdesign.com
www.comstockdesign.com

In-Site Design Group Inc.
1280 South Clayton Street
Denver, CO 80210
(303) 691-9000
insite@insite-design-group.com
www.insite-design-group.com

Kaye Puckett Interior Design
6826 Old Ranch Trail
Littleton, CO 80125
(303) 346-0823
kanddpuckett@comcast.net
www.kayepuckettinteriordesign.com

Top Of The Town Directory.com

In-Site Design Group Inc.
Interior Designer

Phase One Landscapes
Landscape Design

TreeLine Homes, Inc.
Home Builder and Remodeling Contractor

Kitchen Design and Remodel

Kitchen Distributors Inc
1309 West Littleton Boulevard
Littleton, CO 80120
(303) 795-0665
info@kitchendistributors.com
www.kitchendistributors.com

Thurston Kitchen & Bath
2920 East 6th Avenue
Denver, CO 80206
(303) 399-4564
cindy.h@kitchensofcolorado.com
thurstonkitchenandbath.com

Landscape Design

Luxescapes, LLC
9795 Hannibal Court
Commerce City, CO 80022
(303) 288-5893
info@luxescapes.net
www.luxescapes.net

Phase One Landscapes
Landscape Architecture & Construction
2310 South Syracuse Way
Denver, CO 80231
(303) 750-6060
email@phaseonelandscapes.com
www.phaseonelandscapes.com

Landscape Maintenance

Estate Landscape Management
(303) 667-5408
travisrumsey@estate-landscape.com
www.estate-landscape.com

Lighting

Ferguson Bath, Kitchen & Lighting Gallery
17655 East 25th Drive
Aurora, CO 80011
(303) 739-8000
www.ferguson.com

Mortgage Consultant

Cherry Creek Mortgage
Nora Ziel
4845 Pearl East Circle
Boulder, CO 80301
(303) 527-1175
loans@noraziel.com

Colorado Funding Specialists, Inc
Kathy Kokora
4021 West 32nd Avenue
Denver, CO 80212
(303) 507-7728
kokora@msn.com
www.cofunding.com

Colorado State Bank & Trust
Shawn Watts
1600 Broadway
Denver, CO 80202
(303) 861-2111
swatts@csbt.com

Personal Trainer

Mobile Fitness Transformations
3326 South Nelson Street
Lakewood, CO 80227
(720) 261-8854
debbie@mobilefitnesstransformations.com
www.mobilefitnesstransformations.com

Plants, Silk

Beck's Silk Plant Company
Available Thru Your Interior Designer
1111 West Evans Avenue, Suite A-4
Denver, CO 80223
(303) 934-3949
beckssilk@msn.com
www.beckssilkplant.com

Top
Of
The
Town
Directory
.com

Plumbing Fixtures

Euro Bath & Tile
Available Thru Your Trade Professional
475 South Broadway
Denver, CO 80209
(303) 298-8453
www.eurobath-tile.com

Solar Energy

e3 Design Group, Inc.
12150 West 44th Avenue
Wheat Ridge, CO 80033
(303) 908-9770
jimmy@e3designgroupinc.com
www.e3designgroupinc.com

Special Occasion Entertainment

HTR Magic Entertainment
(720) 840-5466
ricardo@magoricardo.com

Sprinkler Services

Altitude Sprinkler & Landscape
(303) 507-9382

Tile

Decorative Materials International Limited
Denver Design District
595 South Broadway, Suite 121E
Denver, CO 80209
(303) 722-1333
allison@decorativematerials.com
www.decorativematerials.com

Euro Bath & Tile
Available Thru Your Trade Professional
475 South Broadway
Denver, CO 80209
(303) 298-8453
www.eurobath-tile.com

Tile and Stone Installation

Geist Flooring
475 West 115th Avenue, Suite 2
Northglenn, CO 80234
(303) 919-4604
geistflooring@yahoo.com
www.geistflooring.com

Window Shutters

Denver Shutter Company
5293 Ward Road, Suite 5
Arvada, CO 80002
(303) 933-3933
chad@denvershuttercompany.com
www.denvershuttercompany.com

Top
Of
The
Town
Directory
.com

VISIONS of DESIGN

An Inspired Collection of North America's Finest Interior Designers

www.tottd.com

Top
Of
The
Town
Directory
.com

VISIONS *of* DESIGN

An Inspired Collection of North America's Finest Interior Designers

Published by

PANACHE
PANACHE PARTNERS, LLC

1424 Gables Court
Plano, TX 75075
469.246.6060
Fax: 469.246.6062
www.panache.com

Publishers: Brian G. Carabet and John A. Shand

Printed in Malaysia

Distributed by Independent Publishers Group
800.888.4741

PUBLISHER'S DATA

Visions of Design

Library of Congress Control Number: 2008932543

ISBN 13: 978-1-933415-67-3
ISBN 10: 1-933415-67-3

First Printing 2008

10 9 8 7 6 5 4 3 2 1

Previous Page: Christine Archer, page 428

This Page: Suzanne Lovell, page 380

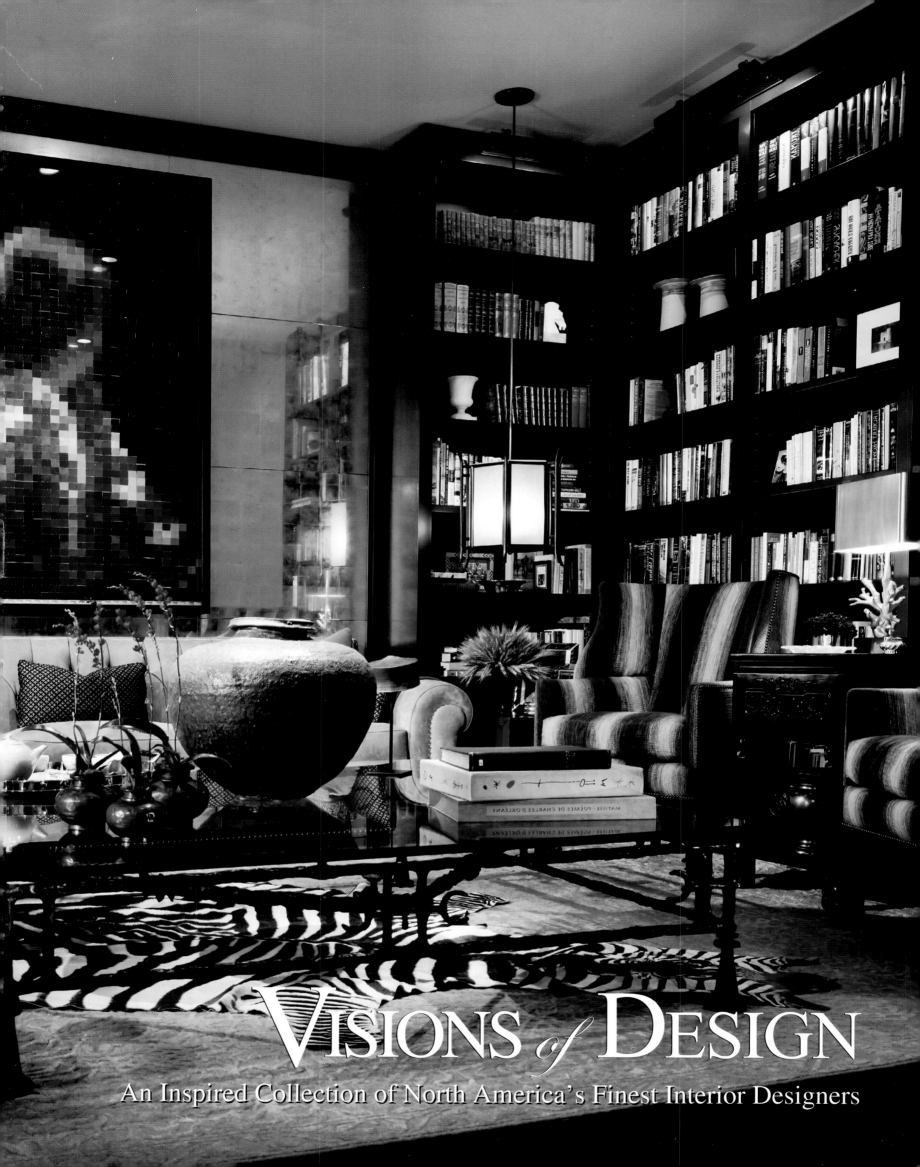

VISIONS *of* DESIGN

An Inspired Collection of North America's Finest Interior Designers

INTRODUCTION

Our individual spaces provide shelter and solace and help shape identity. Our teenage personalities came through the music posters on the walls. In our first apartment, we were proud to have anything that coordinated simply because it was ours. As time passes, the spaces we call home may grow in size or upgrade in location, but one thing remains the same: They are an extension of our character. Good interior design is impressive; great interior design transforms lives.

Visions of Design presents the most talented interior designers across the United States and Canada. Their particular genres are as varied as their backgrounds. Some are former architects, practice interior architecture, or design furniture and textiles. Others integrate their extensive art history backgrounds to design around clients' pieces or help them to establish and grow their collections.

The designers featured among these pages have created awe-inspiring environments for royalty, celebrities, politicians and anyone else with a passion for livable spaces. And while at the top of their industry, these designers never lose touch with functionality, purpose and the all-important client interpretation. The essence of interior design will always be about people and how they live—the reality of what makes for an attractive, civilized, meaningful environment—not fashion or trend. These professionals appreciate all genres of design, constantly raising the standards of their peers and educating their clientele. They view the world from a perspective many can barely comprehend. True talent cannot be learned; it can only be developed and shared.

Glimpse into their powerful interiors of rich, bold color or neutral serenity. Find out what guides their hands and inspires their spaces—in their own words. Each of the four chapters represents a different region of North America. Even if you think you know what each region will bring, *Visions of Design* will open your mind to unimagined possibilities. While traditional style may prevail in New England, talented designers infuse the freshness of contemporary design; while modern may be used with great economy in New York's smaller spaces, classic roots are firmly planted. The doors to exclusive homes are now open. We invite you to come on in.

Brian Carabet & John Shand
Publishers

Facing Page: Lisa Bartolomei, page 20

CONTENTS

Chapter One: Northeast

Above: Arlene Critzos, page 134

Above: Linda Burnside, page 186

Above: James Young, page 482

Chapter Two: Southeast

Above: Marguerite V. Rodgers, page 92

Chapter Three: Midwest

Below: Jorge Castillo, page 362

Above: Paul Vincent Wiseman, page 476

chapter one

chapitre un

capítulo uno

Northeast

Above: Jennifer Post, page 84

Interior design has woven itself throughout the life and pursuits of Barbara Lane for more than three decades and is uniquely complemented by her sincere passion and dedication to philanthropy. Her invaluable contributions to the world of design are seen in numerous projects where her signature contemporary look invites clients into a warm atmosphere. She employs unexpected materials—to keep life interesting with the exciting twists everyone needs—and gently brings depth to even the most challenging spaces. Whether via antique lamps, mirrors or side tables, subtle detailing is paired with clean lines and inevitably produces that unmistakable Barbara Lane essence.

L'architecture intérieure fait partie intégrante de la vie et des entreprises de Barbara Lane depuis plus de trente ans, complétée de manière unique par sa passion sincère pour la philanthropie et son dévouement à cette cause. Ses précieuses contributions au monde du design sont visibles dans de nombreux projets dans lesquels le style contemporain dont elle a fait sa griffe invite les clients dans une ambiance chaleureuse. Elle emploie des matières inattendues pour agrémenter la vie des touches d'originalité passionnantes dont nous avons tous besoin. Elle donne de manière subtile profondeur aux espaces les plus exigeants. Qu'il s'agisse de lampes antiques, de miroirs ou de tables d'appoint, chaque détail subtil est associé à des lignes nettes et permet inévitablement de créer l'essence caractéristique de Barbara Lane.

El diseño de interiores se ha entrelazado en la vida y las actividades de Barbara Lane por más de tres décadas y se complementa de una manera muy especial con su sincera pasión y dedicación a la filantropía. Sus invalorables contribuciones al mundo del diseño se pueden apreciar en numerosos proyectos en los que su característico estilo contemporáneo invita a los clientes a una atmósfera cálida. Hecha mano a materiales inesperados con el objetivo de mantener el interés con los siempre necesarios toques divertidos, y suavemente aportar profundidad aún a los espacios más desafiantes. Ya sea a través de lámparas, espejos o mesas laterales antiguas, los detalles sutiles son combinados con líneas simples que inevitablemente producen la inconfundible esencia de Barbara Lane.

Barbara Lane Interior Design

NEW YORK ■ PARIS

Above: I brought a very modernist mixture of materials into the living room—Plexiglas chairs from the 1970s, a mica and wood mirror, a bronze console and a coffee table made of parchment and Macassar ebony. Contemporary art adds depth to the space, with many thanks to the large-scale pieces of Audrey Hepburn and James Dean.

Right: With the words "go" and "stay" juxtaposed upon these large-scale, romantic photographs, the foyer is given a punch of color and a dash of irony. A young couple wanted a very upbeat space and the Barbara Kruger piece was ideal.

Facing Page: Using Jean Prouvé as the inspiration for the foyer, we cleaned up the space and designed a seating bench with cream and black cowhide pattern. The area mainly functions as a perfect overflow space for cocktail parties since it's positioned between the living and dining rooms as well as the library. Paired with red pillows, the entry space is very graphic and gently complements the limestone floors.

Previous Page: My clients were a young couple who wanted a fresh, young and open apartment. When they first brought me a painting from their contemporary art collection—a Damien Hirst piece hanging now in their dining room—I wasn't instantly fond of it. But after pairing it with an oval red lacquer table and seeing its reflection, I was absolutely stunned. It all combined perfectly with the chandelier by Foscarini and the soup tureen by Cindy Sherman, after Madame Pompadour, bringing a zippy side to the space.
Photographs by Phillip Ennis

Above: For many projects where my clients have young children, I use leather coffee tables to cushion any unavoidable collisions. The media room has a splash of color thanks to its own coffee table, soft red wall color and pony-skin ottomans.

Left: We splashed the naturally glowing guestroom with bright color on the wall and the trundle bed in the center. The couple was able to easily transition the space into a child's room—with built-in storage and desk—when they found out they were expecting.

Facing Page Top & Bottom: Contributing to a soaring contemporary apartment's delicate balance of modernity and elegance is a wall that separates the dining room and library. A mature couple appreciates the round ebony table with parchment base and the feeling it adds to the space. When I first saw the large Thomas Struth photograph of the Milan cathedral, I loved the scale of it and thought it was indicative of the space's purpose: displaying something old within a present-day setting. A wall that doesn't extend to the full height of the ceiling helps the dining room and library function as one space. When I found the stunning Candida Höfer photograph now displayed in the library at an art fair, I bought it. I told my client—a theatre producer—that the perspective in the photo was breathtaking. He loved it and we held it for a year while we waited for the apartment to be finished.
Photographs by Phillip Ennis

"Spaces should flow together and harmoniously infuse the glow of youth with an elegant maturity."

—Barbara Lane

Right: I mixed the old and new within a modern Bulthaup kitchen: An antique chandelier is wrapped in semi-transparent mylar, lighting the linen-covered, oval-shaped breakfast room table.

Facing Page Top: To help my clients' art collection really pop off the wall, I chose a neutral background and sofa. Their four-piece Lee Bai painting is perfectly accompanied by two bronze tables from Paris; the chairs were crafted by Dominique in the 1930s. A total renovation of the couple's Park Avenue apartment yielded an exciting and refreshing ambience to the pre-war space.

Facing Page Bottom: From the comfort of an ultra modern building, breathtaking views of Central Park on the 72nd floor of Time Warner make an inviting space for the residents. We mixed antiques, a bold, blue Yves Klein sculpture and a four-part mica and ebony table with luxurious fabrics. The final product was quite breathtaking—and especially free of clutter. Whenever clients have too much, it's important to edit in order to enjoy the special pieces within the space.
Photographs by Phillip Ennis

Lisa Bartolomei's lifelong interest in art, architecture and antiques inspires her to design unique environments and one-of-a-kind custom furniture for her global clientele. Before turning her attention to residential design, the principal of Bartolomei & Company practiced in the commercial sector, honing her eye for luxury lifestyle venues like fine restaurants, hotels and retail establishments. She sees buying trips to London, Paris, Rome and major cities across the United States as crucial to the design process. Lisa continually expands her vocabulary of ideas, styles and resources to design personalized interiors of a timeless quality.

La passion pour les arts, l'architecture et les antiquités qui anime depuis toujours Lisa Bartolomei inspire ses créations d'environnements et de pièces d'ameublement uniques et exclusives. Avant de se tourner vers la décoration résidentielle, la directrice de Bartolomei & Company a exercé dans le secteur commercial, et s'est familiarisée avec les établissements de luxe tels que des restaurants, hôtels et magasins de détail sophistiqués. Elle considère que les voyages à Londres, Paris, Rome et d'autres villes importantes pour y faire des achats jouent un rôle essentiel dans le cadre du processus de conception. Lisa élargit continuellement son vocabulaire d'idées, de styles et de ressources pour concevoir des intérieurs personnalisés et intemporels.

Su constante pasión por el arte, la arquitectura y las antigüedades sirve de inspiración a Lisa Bartolomei para el diseño de exclusivos entornos y muebles para su clientela global. Antes de dedicarse a pleno al diseño residencial, la directora de Bartolomei & Company ejercía en el sector comercial, desarrollando su apreciación de los ambientes de estilo de vida de lujo, tales como restaurantes, hoteles y establecimientos minoristas de alta gama. Considera que los viajes de compras a Londres, Paris, Roma y grandes ciudades de los Estados Unidos resultan cruciales para el proceso de diseño. Lisa expande continuamente su catálogo de ideas, estilos y recursos para diseñar interiores personalizados de una calidad atemporal.

Lisa Bartolomei

NEW YORK ■ WASHINGTON, D.C.

Above: Dramatic views of the Potomac River are intensified by the warmth of the 1940s' French-inspired living room. I began with the softly patterned carpet and layered textures, natural tones and accents of deep coral. A beautiful 17th-century monk's journal that the couple purchased on their honeymoon in Thailand sits on top of the antique Tibetan chest. The ancient Chinese stone vessels with gold filigree detailing and 1950s' Italian owl lamp add interest and whimsy. A state-of-the-art system allows the residents to open and close the sheer shades and set the lighting to a particular mood at the touch of a button—it's a simple concept but it makes the residents' lives a little more luxurious.

Facing Page Top: I acquired the African fertility gate at an auction and had a rusticated stand built to enhance the physical height, elevating the piece to a work of art more than a mere artifact. The hand-rubbed finish on the dining table and chairs offers a sleek counterpoint, creating a beautiful balance between old and new.

Facing Page Bottom: The moment you enter the bedroom your cares drop away. A tactile combination of creamy ultrasuede, Italian linens, goatskin and rosewood paneling and custom cream-colored lacquer dresser wraps the residents in a cocoon of luxury. Thoughtful details like the closets hidden behind the paneling, and the pop-up television in the dresser—combined with the attention to form and line—create an uncluttered, serene environment.

Previous Page: The project was particularly rewarding because my client was involved in all of the selections and appreciated the level of refinement and detail I gave to the space. Adding the narrow wall to separate the living room from the dining room actually opened the space up and created interesting drama and much better flow. The sycamore bar area conveniently houses three wine refrigerators. When the shades are open, the custom mirror of bronze and nickel reflects the spectacular river view.
Photographs by Geoffrey Hodgdon

Above: Located in a turn-of-the-century building, the contemporary condo was a dramatic change from the owners' previous traditionally furnished Victorian townhouse. They wanted a modern look that would still feel like home, so I exposed them to a wide variety of materials and styles over the course of the project to help them refine their new look. We gutted the interior and built it back up in a modern aesthetic. The bold pattern of the chair inspired the color palette of natural hues with rust, green and aubergine accents.

Right: We found the 1940s' desk by André Sornay in the window of Bernard Goeckler Antiques in New York. It has a sculptural quality and its clean, modernist lines make it an unexpected focal point.

Facing Page: The waterfall provides a Zen-like ambience in both the entrance foyer and the master bathing area cleverly located on the other side. Though the soothing sound of flowing water and the glow of natural light are enjoyed from both spaces, there is complete privacy. The built-in cabinetry was designed as a place to showcase the residents' collection of artwork, including the delightful pre-Columbian figure. A television is concealed within, giving the space great flexibility for events from quiet movie nights to social gatherings.
Photographs by Geoffrey Hodgdon

Top: Design isn't just about creativity, it's also about listening between the lines, because that's where you will find the truth of what people really need—even if they don't know it yet. Initially, a friend I met in yoga class asked for my advice on what flooring she should choose. After quite a bit of conversation, it became clear that flooring alone wouldn't give her the magical effect she was after. She needed a fresh start, a retreat from the world where she could totally unwind at the end of every fast-paced day. The Robert Longo artwork, silk velvet throw pillows, custom Macassar ebony coffee table and ostrich eggs give the space personality. I designed a pedestal to feature the sculpture the woman acquired on a recent trip to Africa, because objects with sentimental value make a place a home, even if everything else in it is totally new. Whether the project is large or small, I spend as much time as it takes to get to know people and help them figure out what they want their home to accomplish. Whether they want a refuge, an entertainment showcase or a family environment, I design every element to work toward that goal.

Bottom: Simple geometry defines the powder room. The strong lines of the wenge and glass vanity are softened by the glow from the nickel and frosted-glass sconces. The walls are a luminescent Venetian plaster.

Facing Page: When I began the design, the gentleman of the house had a very specific yet totally understandable request: at least one comfy chair. He was thrilled to discover that every single seating element in the home is comfortable as well as stylish, especially the luxurious silk mohair sofa I designed. I had the table custom fabricated as well. It's a fairly large rectangle and the legs, which were inspired by the Jazz era, are dense on one end and clear out to reveal just a few curvilinear supports at the far end. The verticality of the coffee table is echoed by the antique French candelabra and the captivating forms of the painting done by Melinda Stickney Gibson, a noted artist and personal friend of mine.
Photographs by Geoffrey Hodgdon

"Design should be a collaborative process of discovery. When homeowners feel empowered, they are more inclined to take an active role in creating their environment."
—Lisa Bartolomei

For Michael Carter, interior design is much like the work of an editor. But instead of a red pen, his listening ear and intuitive eye are the tools that bring shape to his latest design project. And his muse? Antiques, architecture and classical design. As the principal of Carter & Company Interior Design, Michael believes the design process gleans the best from both the designer and client when they operate in a spirit of collaboration and partnership. He offers his discernment and guidance on the most challenging of projects, always maintaining close contact with the highest quality of design resources. With an innate sense of appropriateness and sophistication, Michael weaves an enduring grace into his interiors and focuses on each space's true essence. Quite simply, Carter & Company's timeless design welcomes its residents home time and again.

Pour Michael Carter, l'architecture intérieure est un peu comme l'œuvre d'un réviseur de texte. Au lieu d'un crayon rouge, ce sont son oreille attentive et son œil intuitif qui lui servent d'outils pour donner forme à son dernier projet de design. Ses muses ? Les antiquités, l'architecture et la décoration classiques. À la tête de Carter & Company Interior Design, Michael pense que le processus de création engendre le meilleur de la part du designer comme du client lorsqu'ils travaillent ensemble dans un esprit de collaboration et de partenariat. Les projets les plus difficiles bénéficient toujours de son jugement et de ses conseils. Il entretient toujours un contact étroit avec les ressources de la meilleure qualité en matière de design. Doté d'un sens inné de ce qui est approprié et de la sophistication, Michael infuse ses intérieurs d'une grâce durable et s'attache à mettre en valeur leur essence authentique. Tout simplement, les clients de Carter & Company se sentent toujours chez eux dans son architecture intérieure intemporelle.

Michael Carter sostiene que el diseño de interiores se asemeja considerablemente al trabajo de un editor literario. En lugar de un lápiz rojo, las herramientas que dan forma a su proyecto de diseño actual son su capacidad para escuchar y su intuición. ¿Su musa? Antigüedades, arquitectura y diseño clásico. Como director de Carter & Company Interior Design, Michael considera que el proceso de diseño sintetiza lo mejor tanto del diseñador como del cliente cuando ambos trabajan con un espíritu de cooperación y sociedad. Aporta su discernimiento y guía a los proyectos que representan los mayores desafíos, manteniendo siempre contacto estrecho con los proveedores de diseño de la más alta calidad. Con un sentido innato de adecuación y sofisticación, Michael infunde una elegancia perdurable a sus interiores y se concentra en la esencia verdadera de cada espacio. En pocas palabras, el diseño atemporal de Carter & Company logra una y otra vez que los residentes se sientan en su hogar.

Michael Carter

MASSACHUSETTS

" At its core, good design isn't about style definitions; it's more about artful interpretation."

—Michael Carter

Top: Sometimes it takes a single element to unify a complex space. In the library, it was a classical bust strategically placed in the center of the room. The bust is hollowed out, so when the light from the French doors comes into the room and through the eyes, the face seems to mysteriously come to life.
Photograph by Eric Roth

Bottom: When I first saw the Dessin Fournir mirror, something about it just spoke to me. It is a modern interpretation of a classical convex mirror—a form that has graced Boston mantels for centuries. Here was a perfect opportunity to reinvent a tried-and-true formula in a historic Back Bay brownstone.
Photograph by Eric Roth

Facing Page: Set within an elliptical-shaped living room, the curvilinear doorway that leads out to the conservatory offers an excellent locale for showcasing a replica of *The Winged Victory*. The space's notable ceiling height allows a generous portion of light to intermingle with the room's art, furnishings and function.
Photograph by Sam Gray

Previous Page: To enhance a Boston brownstone's renovation, I chose a soothing palette that would complement the views of its historic, tree-lined street. I was guided by my client's passion for modern art when choosing the foyer's light fixtures; the cube-within-a-cube design is modern yet offset by the hand-wrought nature of the ironwork. Whenever possible, I use classical artifacts and elements in very modern ways—the coffee table legs are based on ancient Greek and Roman design, as are the console table and sculpture.
Photograph by Eric Roth

"Having trust in your designer's taste and integrity—that is the secret to a successful collaboration."

—Michael Carter

Top: A dramatic upholstered headboard with nailhead application in a Nantucket guestroom offers a subtle nod to early 19th-century New England. With an antique bedspread, a modern lamp with a raffia shade, accenting beach glass and shells, the guestroom reflects a fine balance of the old and the new.
Photograph by Michael Lee

Bottom: Since the study has direct views of Nantucket Sound, I definitely chose to work with colors that were evocative of the setting—the sofa fabric is composed of custom-woven, ocean teal-blue chenille. By placing the antique model schooner behind the sofa, it almost appears to be sailing on the horizon with the view out the windows.
Photograph by Michael Lee

Facing Page: Residents of Nantucket revere the island's heritage and hold great respect for its environment—the entirety of my client's home is an authentic expression of its beautiful oceanfront setting. Because the natural surroundings are so important, I made certain that the style of the home remained in harmony by using pared down elements and clean lines, such as the primitive chairs, an antique runner and a simple spiral staircase.
Photograph by Michael Lee

Previous Pages: When I chose a dark, slate color for the walls of the library, it was an attempt to create a dramatic contrast with the lighter objects set within the space. Playing off the room's theme, I designed the chaise lounges to resemble book ends. My fondness for classical design can be seen in the architectural Venetian mirror over the mantel, and in an inset Greek key border on the floor, with a similar design on the sides of the desk and chair. To blend in some modern elements, I enclosed an 18th-century Italian gilt wood chandelier in a cubed linen shade, thereby adding contrast to the dark ceiling and also bringing a wonderful sense of geometry to the space.
Photograph by Eric Roth

There is a distinct psychology in the way people look at things. The designer arts—whether fashion or interior—can be thought of as one big puzzle, where the elements flow together for a cohesive whole. As Alex Clymer made the transition from fashion to interior design, she discovered this connection and realized that you can design in many ways, as long as the design infuses the needs and desires of the client. Alex founded her design firm, Alex Clymer Interiors, based on this principle. This is where true success exists: in the realm of timelessness, when a visitor walks into the room and sees the homeowners' personality, not the designer's. Alex Clymer is an exceptional designer, who believes it is imperative that each client's individual visions and expectations are attained. Consequently, she is an excellent listener whose approach is to make the design journey all about the client. Alex is a designer with integrity, bringing passion and unique sensibility to each and every project.

La façon dont les gens perçoivent les choses relève de leurs psychologies distinctes. L'art du designer, qu'il s'agisse de mode ou de décoration intérieure, peut être conçu comme un grand puzzle, dont les éléments s'articulent pour former un ensemble cohérent. Lorsque Alex Clymer est passée de la mode à la décoration, elle a découvert cette connexion et a compris que l'on peut décorer de nombreuses manières différentes, à condition que l'œuvre du designer s'inspire des besoins et désirs du client. Alex a fondé son cabinet d'architecture intérieure, Alex Clymer Interiors, en s'appuyant sur ce principe. C'est là que réside la véritable réussite : dans le domaine de l'intemporel, lorsqu'un visiteur rentre dans une pièce et y reconnaît la personnalité de son propriétaire, et non celle du décorateur. Alex Clymer est une décoratrice exceptionnelle, qui est convaincue qu'il est impératif de respecter la vision et les attentes individuelles de chaque client. Elle fait donc preuve d'excellentes qualités d'écoute et le client reste au centre de son travail. Alex est une décoratrice caractérisée par une grande intégrité, dont la passion et la sensibilité unique transparaissent dans chacune des œuvres.

Existe una psicología particular en la manera en que las personas contemplan las cosas. Es posible considerar a las artes de diseño, ya sea de moda o de interiores, como un gran rompecabezas en el que los elementos fluyen para formar un todo cohesivo. A medida que Alex Clymer llevó a cabo la transición desde el diseño de moda al de interiores, descubrió dicha conexión y aprendió que es posible diseñar de diversas maneras, siempre y cuando el diseño infunda las necesidades y deseos del cliente. Alex fundó su compañía de diseño, Alex Clymer Interiors, en base a ese principio. Es justamente ahí donde existe el verdadero éxito: en el reino de lo atemporal, cuando un visitante entra a una habitación y reconoce la personalidad de su propietario, no la del diseñador. Alex Clymer es una diseñadora excepcional, que considera que es imperativo que se materialicen las visiones y expectativas individuales de cada cliente. Por lo tanto, escucha cuidadosamente y su enfoque consiste en desarrollar el proceso de diseño centrado en el cliente. Alex es una diseñadora con integridad, que aporta pasión y una sensibilidad única a cada proyecto.

Alex Clymer

MARYLAND

Above: After renovating other rooms, the existing kitchen no longer flowed with the rest of the house. The homeowners wanted the gourmet kitchen to be the heart of their home, especially since they love to cook and entertain. The space presented several challenges, being longer than wider and deficient in natural light. By replacing the flat-paned windows with custom window boxes, the desired light, depth and charm were achieved. The 16-foot island, with its thick mahogany top, helps the room appear wider and creates two distinct areas that allow the cooks to be part of the mix, while entertaining their guests.

Right & Previous Page: The shoreline residence, with its breathtaking views, is an absolute sanctuary. Incorporating an abundance of architectural and multitextural details, it is a blend of casual, livable luxury, befitting the lifestyle of the clients. Through the combined efforts of everyone involved, the residence was given the utmost attention. Hand-selected walnut wood was used on the wainscoted walls and floors. Fieldstone accented several walls. A natural stone floor was used in the foyer and other areas. This is design integrity at its best.

Facing Page: The breakfast room was renovated along with the kitchen. When designing the room, the dry-walled ceiling was typically flat and lacked character. We agreed that by altering the pitch of the ceiling and adding distressed wood, the desired look would be achieved. The antique chandelier—a cherished find by the homeowners—became our statement piece. We further embraced the Tuscan charm by utilizing other textural elements.
Photographs by Gordon Beall

Above & Left: The multifunctional space harmoniously serves as a music room, a gallery and a place to replenish one's spirit. The monochromatic palette creates a tranquil backdrop for the blending of various periods and styles. Imported hand-gilded and finished moulding with antique mirror lends itself to the echoing of color and light. Murals painted on the ceiling add a touch of the unexpected. The setting transcends time with an opulence that plays on and on.
Photographs by John Coyle

Facing Page Top: Beautifully blending soft tones and various textures, this dining room conveys a quiet drama. The glittering tablescape is a mixture of china, crystal and sterling flatware. The clients are free to create the mood of the seasons as it suits their whims.
Photograph by Alan Gilbert

Facing Page Bottom: Glazed walls and a washed, stenciled, Venetian plaster ceiling add a dimension to the otherwise nondescript room. Small but inviting, the room is positioned across the foyer from the dining room. An eclectic mix of clean lines and styles helps to make the room flow easily with the surrounding spaces.
Photograph by Alan Gilbert

" All of our designs are about living, for design
is a necessary luxury."

—Alex Clymer

Right: Custom drapery completes the total look. Coverings should be
designed to fit the space and help create the mood of the room. We
never skimp on workmanship. Two exquisite fabrics were sewn together
to create a restrained richness without adding heaviness. Cording,
crystal beading and large tassels, along with the decorative hardware,
interplay with the surrounding details.

Facing Page Top: The bedroom, overlooking a lush landscape with
resort-style pool and spa, fulfills the clients' wish for a palette
with punches of fresh, crisp and current colors. The custom window
treatments were designed to allow light to flow in while providing some
privacy. By painting the multifaceted ceiling as a fifth wall, a sense of
envelopment was attained, pulling the look together.

Facing Page Bottom: Dining rooms are about good food, good wine
and, most of all, good company. The clients wanted comfort in their
seating and so we used the wonderful settee. The crown moulding and
wainscoting are antiques to give Old World charm. The walls, painted in
a soft golden shade, serve as a perfect backdrop for the homeowners'
artwork, while the metallic fauxed ceiling adds to the ambience.
Photographs by Gordon Beall

Give Brian Gluckstein one glimpse at a home's bare bones, and he'll immediately start redefining the space. It's not just the aesthetic presentation of a home that his skill identifies, but its very heart and functional efficiency, too. Ceilings open, straight stairs curve and dark corners brighten once his designer's eye for detail has found the home's greater purpose. Brian's designs achieve a mastered timelessness no matter the period or culture they reflect; but one element they all share is obvious: innovation. His solutions are far from status quo and often surprise both homeowners and their guests. With his commitment to livable designs, excellence is the key factor that echoes through each finished project by Gluckstein Design.

Il suffit de permettre à Brian Gluckstein de jeter un seul coup d'œil sur la seule structure d'une maison, et il commence immédiatement à en redéfinir l'espace. Ce n'est pas seulement la présentation esthétique d'une résidence qu'il met en valeur, mais également son cœur même et son efficacité fonctionnelle. Les plafonds s'ouvrent, les escaliers droits s'incurvent, et les coins sombres s'éclairent dès que le sens du détail du décorateur a identifié la raison d'être plus profonde de la maison. Les œuvres de Brian sont marquées par la maîtrise d'un caractère intemporel, quelle que soit la période ou la culture dont elles s'inspirent. Elles s'articulent toutefois toutes autour d'un élément commun : l'innovation. Ses solutions s'écartent largement du statu quo et surprennent souvent à la fois les propriétaires des résidences et leurs invités. Il entend concevoir des espaces conviviaux, marqués par l'excellence de tous les projets finis par Gluckstein Design.

Brian Gluckstein sólo requiere una breve mirada a la estructura de un hogar para comenzar inmediatamente a redefinir el espacio. Sus habilidades identifican no sólo la presentación estética de un hogar, también alcanzan su corazón y su eficiencia funcional. Una vez que el ojo para los detalles de este diseñador ha encontrado su fin último, los cielorrasos se abren, las escaleras rectas se vuelven curvas y los rincones oscuros se iluminan. Los diseños de Brian logran una cualidad atemporal independientemente del periodo o cultura que reflejan; pero uno de los elementos en común resulta evidente: la innovación. Sus soluciones escapan al status quo y frecuentemente sorprenden tanto a los propietarios como a sus visitas. Con su compromiso con los diseños habitables, la excelencia constituye un factor clave que se repite en cada proyecto terminado de Gluckstein Design.

Brian Gluckstein

Above: I strove to design the bathroom in a style that would be an extension of the entire home. In order to make it feel more like a relaxation space, I avoided traditional bathroom fixtures and featured custom-designed furniture. The vanity/sink was made as a chest of draws, and lamps were chosen instead of wall sconces; an original Deco table rests beside the cast iron bathtub. In the center of the room is a marble mosaic with a marble border, giving the illusion of a carpet set beneath the custom-designed terrycloth chairs.

Facing Page: Since the home was designed in an established neighborhood of traditional houses, I designed the kitchen to reflect a style from the earlier part of the 20th century. Architectural details within the traditional, painted frame kitchen were made to honor the space's historical depth. I mixed some contemporary elements such as the marble wall over the sink and floating marble shelves with antique glass cabinets and traditional hardware. Within a very grand, large-scale house, the kitchen achieved a cozy ambience with its bright palette and dark hardwood floors.

Previous Page: In order to give an urban penthouse's living space a sophisticated loft feel, I designed it to be a clean, contemporary environment. What's notable about the space is its ability to age very well. Dramatic walnut cabinets contrasted with a silk carpet and chrome Deco-inspired chairs—these elements are just a few that display the room's luxurious modernity. I placed a light linen fabric behind the open display cabinets in order to lighten the space and not detract attention from the artifacts.
Photographs by Ted Yarwood

Above Left & Right: A beautiful Tudor house's staircase flows through all three stories, and in order to give it a distinct richness, I chose stained wall paneling in pine and an iron railing. For the second-floor landing, I decided that the two-story library would be a dramatic and out-of-the-ordinary design option for my client's book collection. With such a tall space, I lessened its intimidating scale by using a wide crown moulding between the two stories and also by giving a third-floor bedroom a set of French doors overlooking the space; two-story linen drapes soften the space and help with acoustical needs. Oatmeal-colored furnishings allow the books, antique carpet and artifacts to be the room's focal point.

Left: To give the Deco-inspired room a distinct contrast, I upholstered the walls in a masculine, lightly colored leather and used dark wood shelving. Among the linens, mohair and velvet fabrics, I wanted something that was eye-catching, crisp and clean—a painting of an old camera was a natural fit and gives the room a discernible freshness.

Facing Page: I brought my clients' traditional home into the 21st century by carefully juxtaposing classic architecture and contemporary furnishing. A French 19th-century gilded table is set between two Deco arm chairs and in front of a nickel Deco floor lamp. I thoroughly enjoyed the process of balancing an eclectic mixture of furniture to modernize the very traditional house, while also infusing it with a lovely timelessness.
Photographs by Ted Yarwood

Top & Bottom: If everyone had such a Zen-like bathroom, we'd never make it to work! Centered around a Japanese garden-inspired atrium, the undeniable focal point of the entire space is its infinity bathtub—which overflows into a trough to re-heat and then re-enter the main tub with a nearby marble chaise and terrycloth cushion. Floating in front of a frosted window is an ebony shelf for bath products and candles; the adjacent mirror actually conceals a television. I was also inspired to make the showering experience indicative of outdoor bathing and chose to connect the shower to the outdoor atrium; teak deck flooring and a set of floating showerheads contribute to the one-of-a-kind area.

Facing Page: The main hall of the house was originally quite long, so I chose to break it into a series of spaces by creating deep, paneled archways that serve as separate entrances into the home's various rooms. Complementing the beautiful mouldings is a limestone floor, which I specified in a brick pattern in order to give the effect of an old European floor. To give the spaces some added definition, I hung lanterns in each archway.
Photographs by Ted Yarwood

Evoking a timeless sophistication in her clients' homes, Barbara Kotzen of Tappe & Kotzen Interior Design blends customized designs with architectural features. Styles range from casually elegant and traditional to transitional and contemporary. With each project she focuses on every detail, from custom millwork and cabinetry to the finishing touches in furniture, draperies, rugs, custom trims and wall colors. Barbara's dedication to functional design is seamlessly expressed so that every home is an extension of her clients' personality and lifestyle. Her meticulous attention to each element in a room creates a beautiful harmony and balance throughout the space, which has become the notable signature in all her work.

Barbara Kotzen de Tappe & Kotzen Interior Design donne aux résidences de ses clients une sophistication intemporelle, et associe des dessins personnalisés aux éléments architecturaux. Les styles de ces œuvres vont de l'élégance informelle et traditionnelle au contemporain et au transitionnel. Elle s'attache à chaque détail de chaque projet, de la menuiserie intérieure et des placards aux touches de finition du mobilier, aux rideaux, aux tapis, en passant par les boiseries personnalisées et les couleurs des murs. L'enthousiasme de Barbara pour une conception fonctionnelle s'exprime de manière harmonieuse de sorte que chaque résidence est un prolongement de la personnalité et du style de vie de ses clients. L'attention méticuleuse qu'elle porte à chaque élément permet l'instauration d'une harmonie et d'un équilibre magnifiques dans l'ensemble de l'espace, une caractéristique notable qui ressort comme la marque de ses œuvres.

Evocando una sofisticación atemporal en los hogares de sus clientes, Barbara Kotzen, de Tappe & Kotzen Interior Design, combina diseños personalizados con detalles arquitectónicos. Los estilos van desde la elegancia casual y tradicional a lo transicional y contemporáneo. En cada proyecto se concentra en cada uno de los detalles, desde la carpintería y gabinetes personalizados a los toques de terminación en los muebles, cortinas, alfombras, terminaciones personalizadas y colores de las paredes. Su dedicación al diseño funcional se expresa fluidamente, de manera que cada hogar constituye una extensión de la personalidad y estilo de vida de sus clientes. Su meticulosa atención a cada elemento en una habitación crea una bella armonía y balance en todo el espacio, que se ha convertido en una característica notable de todos sus trabajos.

Barbara Kotzen

MASSACHUSETTS

Above: A Tudor estate in a suburb of Boston became the canvas for an exceptional renovation that transformed the home into a masterpiece melding function and elegance. The comfortable yet graceful side room extending from the main living room is a perfect example. French doors open to an enclosed porch with stone columns and a beamed ceiling to extend the living space.

Left: Reclaimed oak floors were used through the entire house to complement the ornate paneling and provide continuity. Custom-designed Tibetan area rugs on the floors offer elements of color and texture. A leaded window alcove in the family room serves as a perfect area for the game table and a unique place to admire the grounds of the property.

Facing Page Left & Right: After living in England for eight years, my clients dreamed of an area reminiscent of an English phone booth. The floorplan was modified and a powder room covered in glass tiles from floor to ceiling was incorporated beneath the stairs. Strategically placed mirrors mimic a phone booth's windows. With a mosaic of the Queen's crown, a glass-etched sink, crystal handle faucets and custom-tole light, the ornate space embodies the grandeur of royalty.

Previous Page: An original Liechtenstein masterpiece was among the homeowners' favorites in their collection and naturally became the anchor of the living room. Since the color palette was fairly bold, deep blue and caramel colors were used to complement the art. A Tibetan rug rests beneath the intricately carved coffee table and armchairs. Custom trim along the bottom of the sofa and pillows contributes to the overall color palette and texture. The balance of scale in the room creates depth, which draws the eye toward the artwork.
Photographs by Sam Gray Photography

Above: A Utah guest home has the perfect view overlooking the Wasatch Mountains. Not only does the living room provide a comfortable gathering place with its leather ottoman and striped Tibetan rug, but it also offers a space for the owner—an excellent sportsman—to display his accomplishments.

Facing Page Top: To create a cozy feeling, the dining area is combined with an informal family room. Rich fabrics and textures add wonderful warmth to the space. Large windows with custom millwork provide a frame for spotting wildlife on the mountain.

Facing Page Left & Right: The entry of the house greets guests with slate stone and metal leaf accents, which introduces the theme of nature that is carried throughout the home. I used organic materials abundantly, as is evidenced in the post and beam work down the hallway and the paneling of the study. Chairs upholstered in zebra-striped velvet evoke a sense of the wild and feel at home with the artwork and accessories in the room. The home becomes a comfortable retreat for its many guests.
Photographs by Sam Gray Photography

Top: The formal dining room embodies elegance and sophistication with rich textiles, an ornate silk rug and a delicate crystal chandelier. The fabric used for the dining chairs was custom-designed to harmonize with the colors of the red grass-cloth wall covering and the chocolate velvet drapes. A unique mirror provides a beautiful reflection of the depth and balance in the space.

Bottom: Clean lines of the draperies and furniture work well to complement the graceful pattern of the wallpaper in the master bedroom. The color palette of greens and blues provides the light, crisp feel of the seaside found in the oil painting from the homeowners' collection. The room is complete with custom trim on the lampshades and luxurious bed linens.

Facing Page: To provide contrast to the bright yellow walls in this living room, I selected dark wood furniture and a diverse array of textiles. The antique armchairs framing the fireplace are upholstered with a dynamic pink velvet. Custom tasseled trim on the pillows and draperies are just a few of the details that add to the lively ambience of the space.
Photographs by Sam Gray Photography

"Throughout the design process I carefully consider every detail— from texture and scale to color and lighting—to create an atmosphere that truly becomes an extension of my client's personality."

—Barbara Kotzen

A contemplative designer with a stellar reputation for creating unique interiors throughout Toronto and internationally, Ariel Muller cares most about satisfying his clients' lifestyle needs and desires. With strict adherence to proven architectural principles, he works in all genres designing exquisite environments that combine custom fabrications using interesting woods and metals, luxurious textiles, fine appointments and personal art collections. Ariel's eye for melding classic elements with modern accents is masterful, while his sensitivity to function, comfort and integrating the most current technologies is apparent the moment one enters his meticulously designed spaces.

Ariel Muller, un décorateur contemplatif brillamment réputé pour les intérieurs uniques qu'il a créés à Toronto et au niveau international, est surtout préoccupé par les besoins et les désirs de ses clients compte tenu de leur style de vie. Il respecte strictement des principes d'architecture éprouvés, et travaille dans tous les genres pour concevoir des cadres exquis qui associent des fabrications personnalisées à l'aide de bois et métaux, des textiles luxueux, des meubles raffinés et des collections d'art personnelles. Le sens aigu d'Ariel pour la fusion d'éléments classiques et de nuances modernes est impressionnant, et sa sensibilité à la fonction, au confort et à l'intégration des technologies les plus innovantes est apparente dès que l'on entre dans ses espaces méticuleusement pensés.

Un diseñador contemplativo con una reputación estelar por la creación de interiores exclusivos en Toronto e internacionalmente, Ariel Muller se preocupa principalmente de satisfacer las necesidades de estilo de vida y los deseos de sus clientes. Con una estricta adhesión a principios arquitectónicos probados, trabaja en todos los géneros diseñando entornos exquisitos que combinan fabricaciones personalizadas utilizando maderas y metales interesantes, textiles y mobiliario de lujo y colecciones de arte personales. Posee una magistral habilidad para fusionar elementos clásicos con detalles modernos; su preocupación por la función, la comodidad y la integración de las últimas tecnologías queda al descubierto en cuanto se ingresa a uno de sus espacios meticulosamente diseñados.

Ariel Muller

Above: Strong yet inviting, the combination of artfully moulded stone, forged metal ironwork, copper fixtures and earthen-hued velvet drapery exudes serene, natural elegance.

Right: An inviting rustic ambience is reflected throughout the home; a custom console with framed oversized mirror enhances the hallway and opens up the space.

Facing Page Top: A great room's warmth defies its impressive scale. Soaring ceilings and expansive views mesh with welcoming seating areas and rich wood tones for the ultimate log home experience combining comfort and luxury.

Facing Page Bottom: Nestled under the mezzanine and anchoring an expansive great room, the double-island kitchen with bespoke cabinetry and granite elements deftly conceals appliances, thus preserving function without sacrificing form.

Previous Page: We designed a handcrafted bubinga wood dining table with comfortable espresso leather and chenille chairs to meld with the chocolate brown reclaimed elm floors. The handsome presentation of rustic grandeur is reminiscent of a stately lodge.

Photographs by John Trigiani

"Formality and practicality can coexist."

—Ariel Muller

Above: We created a concert of classical details to draw people in. A sophisticated rosewood Steinway piano is complemented by refined accents, including antique glass drapery finials, luxuriously tactile fabrics and an exquisite Chihuly glass centerpiece.

Facing Page Top: Enveloped by tufted silk chairs and paneled walls, the grand sapele pommele wood table mirrors an oval-domed classical ceiling, creating an elegant dining atmosphere.

Facing Page Bottom: The vaulted great room uses veiled technology, graceful chandeliers and generous seating to provide a versatile gathering space. Its classical lines and family-friendly appointments combine traditional good looks with livability.
Photographs by David Whittaker

"The greatest pleasure is working with people and bringing out their tastes, preferences and desires."

—Ariel Muller

Top: From the curvilinear anigre wood bar to the modern stools, fluid lines mimic the captivating saltwater aquarium to provide a casual-chic food and wine setting.
Photograph by John Trigiani

Center: Quiet moments call for a natural stone fireplace with organic wood mantel complemented by custom chairs and an artisan burlwood and bronze coffee table.
Photograph by John Trigiani

Bottom: Creating drama in a modern space, an uplit onyx counter is supported by its figured anigre wood vanity with a custom bronze vessel.
Photograph by David Whittaker

Facing Page Top: Seamlessly merging form and function, the media room's classic contemporary aesthetic creates a cocooning effect through natural elements and carefully concealed technology.
Photograph by David Whittaker

Facing Page Bottom: Surrounded by hand-chiseled stone walls, the infinity tub's continuously cascading water cultivates an air of tranquility in the master ensuite retreat.
Photograph by John Trigiani

A former art teacher, Suzanne Novik believes that art is everywhere—one need only look outside to see the way textures and colors converge to produce harmonious landscapes. Suzanne finds inspiration outdoors in colors and patterns and creates interiors with a constant visual flow from the outside in. She also designs for continuity between rooms: At the beginning of a design project she collaborates with the client to select a theme to tie each room together, such as a soft neutral color, which will appear in varying forms in rooms throughout the home. Since opening her namesake firm in 1994, Suzanne has worked with a wide variety of satisfied clientele to design elegant rooms that embody their specific purpose. She maintains that great interior design enables a home to function as a three-dimensional sculpture one can move through—just like nature, art is everywhere.

Suzanne Novik est un ancien professeur d'art et pense que celui-ci se trouve partout. Il suffit de regarder à l'extérieur pour observer la convergence des textures et couleurs pour produire des paysages harmonieux. Suzanne s'inspire des couleurs et motifs de la nature pour créer des intérieurs caractérisés par un flux visuel ininterrompu de l'extérieur vers l'intérieur. Elle s'attache également dans ces conceptions à la continuité entre les pièces. Au début d'un projet de décoration, elle collabore avec le client pour choisir un thème commun à toutes les pièces, comme une couleur douce et neutre, qui apparaîtra sous différentes formes dans l'ensemble de la maison. Depuis la fondation de l'entreprise qui porte son nom en 1994, Suzanne travaille avec une clientèle variée et satisfaite pour concevoir des pièces élégantes adaptées à leur objet spécifique. Pour elle, une grande architecture intérieure permet à la résidence de fonctionner comme une sculpture en trois dimensions dans laquelle on peut se déplacer, tout comme dans la nature, l'art est partout.

Suzanne Novik, una ex profesora de arte, está convencida de que el arte es omnipresente. Sólo es necesario mirar a nuestro alrededor para observar la manera en que las texturas y colores se combinan para producir paisajes armoniosos. Suzanne encuentra su inspiración al aire libre, en los colores y patrones, y crea interiores con un flujo visual constante desde el exterior. Su diseño busca además la continuidad entre habitaciones: Al comienzo de un proyecto de diseño colabora con el cliente en la selección de un tema en común para cada habitación, tal como un color neutro suave, que aparecerá de diversas formas en las habitaciones del hogar. Desde la creación de la compañía que lleva su nombre en 1994, Suzanne ha trabajado con una amplia variedad de clientes satisfechos para diseñar habitaciones elegantes que representan su propósito específico. Sostiene que los grandes diseñadores de interiores hacen posible que un hogar funcione como una escultura tridimensional por la que podemos desplazarnos. Al igual que la naturaleza, el arte es omnipresente.

Suzanne Novik

Above: A departure from the owners' more formal residence in Connecticut, the New Hampshire home's natural aesthetic blends harmoniously with the rustic setting and every room has a lake view. The loft is designed to resemble a library and includes a large custom-made bookcase displaying a collection of antique books and accessories indigenous to the area. Inviting chairs around an ottoman complete the peaceful reading area.
Photograph by Pam Soorenko, Photogroup

Facing Page: The living room of a Japanese-style New York apartment is a place of tranquility. Acquired from a Japanese art gallery, the painting dictates the neutral colors and establishes a serene mood as gold, gray, pale terracotta and sage colors set the room's theme. Two chairs in a geometric dotted gold on gray background complement the rug, which is also gray and gold albeit in a more linear geometric motif. Luxurious velvet pillows of floral gold, gray and terracotta accent the gray mohair sofa. The black wood of the cocktail table, sofa and chairs complement the granite countertops and balance with the painting's dark tree trunk.
Photograph by Pam Soorenko, Photogroup

Previous Page: Truly meant to be, I found my dream home on the first day of my search when I relocated to the Westport/Weston area in 1994; it was previously owned by a woman who had my maiden name. In designing the new rooms and areas, I wanted to utilize the numerous pieces of furniture and accessories inherited from my parents' and grandparents' collections. The family room's masculine theme was inspired by a quilt I had made from my father's vast collection of roughly 350 ties and the space includes reclaimed barn wood floors, ceiling beams and a stone fireplace. The compelling game table is made from hickory tree trunk with an Australian lace wood top.
Photograph by Chi Chi Ubiña

"The results best reflect the client's personal style when design expertise is blended with strong attention to detail."

—Suzanne Novik

Above: The guest suite is a tribute to my mother, whose favorite color was blue. The room is perched atop a staircase and I fondly refer to the ascent as "climbing the stairs to heaven." I wanted to recreate the feeling of a space like my grandmother's attic yet imbue it with a celestial aura, which was achieved through the use of a palette of primarily whites and accents of pale blue. By using the reverse side of the fabrics in some of the pillows and the headboard I instilled an aged look. Flanking the bed are Victorian tables painted a crisp white, which complement the headboard's Victorianesque lines. The rug is angled to keep the look informal and exhibit more of the floor.
Photograph by Chi Chi Ubiña

Facing Page Top: I designed the space for the Kinderwood Showhouse as a dressing room since there was a large built-in armoire and an adjoining walk-in closet, and my inspiration came from my mother's collection of vintage hats, suits and accessories. The window treatment resembles a theater drape behind a custom-designed, mirrored dressing table. The tray ceiling upholstered in light pink-gold lamé reflects the light from an antique Steuben glass fixture hanging below. The ceiling is adorned with wallpaper patterned with gold stars against a pale pink background; black-and-white photos of vintage movie stars against a palette of blush tones complete the ambience.
Photograph by Pam Soorenko, Photogroup

Facing Page Bottom: Allowing family and friends to gather in one big space, I met my client's entertaining desires by designing this area such that the living room is open to the dining room to facilitate large groups. To further accommodate larger gatherings, the seating arrangement can be removed and replaced with an expansive dining table and chairs, but the current arrangement works well for smaller, intimate get-togethers. The homeowner's love of yellow is reflected in the space, which is light-filled thanks to three French doors with western exposures.
Photograph by Pam Soorenko, Photogroup

Top: The immaculate Empire-style chandelier was the perfect find for the light-filled hallway, which is scaled exquisitely with the plaster ceiling medallion. The iron balustrade is gilded to add just the right touch of formality; antique interior prints cascade down the spiral staircase, creating rhythm and natural flow to the space.

Bottom: Surrounded by wonderful French doors adorned with white and yellow drapes, the antique clock exudes elegance in the combination living room-dining room where the elegant settee beckons one to enjoy a moment of repose.

Facing Page: A pair of oval gold leaf mirrors with a sunflower motif, which came from the client's previous master bath, inspired the sophisticated yet whimsical theme for the master bathroom. The floral theme is enhanced via 20th-century rock crystal sconces with amber and clear crystal flowers; vintage amber buttons add the perfect touch to the resplendent balloon shade.
Photographs by Pam Soorenko, Photogroup

"By establishing one-of-a-kind artistic formations of space that incorporate my clients' specific needs, I create home environments that flow with a sense of balance and harmony."
—Suzanne Novik

For more than three decades Barbara Ostrom Associates has designed an array of singular, intimately tailored spaces for high-end clients around the world. Working closely with homeowners Barbara creates warmth and comfortable elegance through beautiful colors and vibrant décor. However, her renowned designs eschew recognition as each space represents the personality and unique tastes of the particular client. Working with clean, contemporary designs as well as those of an intricate, highly detailed aesthetic, she considers every design aspect, from mouldings to woodworking to gazebos and verandas—truly all architectural elements are explored and often created from scratch to complete the perfect design.

Depuis plus de trente ans, Barbara Ostrom Associates conçoit des espaces singuliers et intimement personnalisés destinés à des clients de haut de gamme dans le monde entier. Fruits d'une étroite collaboration avec les propriétaires des maisons, les créations de Barbara, avec leurs couleurs magnifiques et vibrantes, sont empreintes d'une élégance chaleureuse et confortable. Ses œuvres sont connues pour leur prise en compte de la personnalité et des goûts uniques de chaque client particulier. Elle travaille avec des conceptions sobres, contemporaines, ainsi qu'avec des esthétiques complexes et très détaillées, et prend en compte chaque aspect de la décoration, des moulures à l'ébénisterie, en passant par les pavillons de jardin et les vérandas. Tous les éléments architecturaux sans exception sont explorés et souvent créés de toute pièce pour obtenir une décoration parfaite.

Durante más de tres décadas, Barbara Ostrom Associates ha diseñado una variedad de singulares espacios íntimamente adaptados para clientes de alta gama de todo el mundo. En estrecha cooperación con los propietarios, Barbara crea calidez y elegancia confortable a través de bellos colores y una decoración vibrante. Sin embargo, sus famosos diseños evitan la repetición, ya que cada espacio representa la personalidad y los gustos exclusivos de cada cliente en particular. Trabajando con diseños simples y contemporáneos y también con aquellos de una estética intrincada y altamente detallada, Barbara toma en cuenta cada aspecto de diseño, desde las molduras hasta la carpintería, los gazebos y las galerías. Todos los elementos arquitectónicos son explorados y frecuentemente creados de la nada para completar el diseño perfecto.

Barbara Ostrom

Above & Right: From a dark bar we created a bright kitchen for a contemporary home in The Hamptons, and opened up an entire wall with glass, bringing ocean views inside; the custom-made canvas fan with lighting creates the most wonderful breezes when the doors are open. We designed a charming banquette dining area that is a favorite of the owners.

Facing Page Top & Bottom: In an older house with many antiques the desire was for a bright, uplifting ambience. Exquisite antiques and Waterford crystal chandeliers say formal, but wall coverings handpainted in China in hues of deep orange and hot pink, dazzling silk draperies from France and vibrantly colored, alternating chair seats exude a playful aura. The owners love the light and flowery seating area we made in the window niche.

Previous Page: We treated the solarium in an unexpected way: high-gloss, red Chinese lacquer walls are adorned with grosgrain ribbon fastened with nailheads in a Chippendale design; an eclectic mix of French, Chinese and contemporary furniture ideally suits the airy, effervescent room. Andrew Tedesco painted the ceiling with flying birds, sky and a continuation of palms. *Photographs by Phillip Ennis*

Above & Left: The addition of the veranda to a home in Greenwich, Connecticut, united two wings of the house and created a private terrace upstairs for the bedroom. The owners wanted the effect of a room that could also withstand the elements; the furniture can get rained on while the tile floor endures both freezing and sweltering conditions, and the elegant antique statues function as gaslights.

Facing Page: A renovation called for a scaling down of the kitchen; we created a charming breakfast spot by taking out an existing wall to the laundry area, which we framed with an impressive Spanish-Portuguese arch. Tile adorns both floor and ceiling in a light-filled room with many antiques; the frescoed walls further procure a Mediterranean feel.
Photographs by Phillip Ennis

"No single element applies to all clients. People are different and eclectic within themselves."
—Barbara Ostrom

Top, Center & Bottom: The owners of a New York City triplex lived for many in years in Portugal and wanted to recreate its unique essence at home; they brought back containers of exquisite Portuguese tile that were just perfect. We designed the beams and all interior architecture. We tore down a wall separating two rooms and the space opens onto a terrace with French doors of expansive glass, creating a rustic, flower- and plant-filled setting of joy and respite.

Facing Page Top & Bottom: We built an extraordinary conservatory and closed off an entire New York City street to hoist it atop a barren rooftop, creating an ethereal, aromatic escape for the owners of a contemporary townhouse. A complete departure from the interior's monochromatic aesthetic, the garden is filled with many of the clients' antiques from travels, plants, flowers and an array of enchanting birds. *Photographs by Phillip Ennis*

World-renowned Manhattan interior architect and designer Jennifer Post has been part of the modern minimalist yet elegant space design movement for decades—and is today one of the genre's most gifted devotees. Extremely passionate about the approach she calls classic and sophisticated, Jennifer achieves design purity through clean, fresh design. Her spaces have transformed even traditionalists into minimalists. Light floods each environment, creating qualities of serenity and warmth—a crucial juxtaposition to her clients' busy lives. Spaces encompassing strong architectural elements, clean lines, tailored furnishings, and neutral hues punctuated by dramatic color are Jennifer Post's high-demand signature. A waiting list attests to the success Jennifer believes comes from her ability to listen and thusly reflect her clients' tastes, desires and needs; she educates those who want her look—they are a very sophisticated clientele. A high-energy businesswoman with the heart of a true artist, Jennifer aspires to awe all who experience her interiors.

Jennifer Post, architecte d'intérieur et décoratrice de Manhattan réputée dans le monde entier, adhère depuis plusieurs dizaines d'années au mouvement minimaliste sans rien perdre d'élégance de la décoration de l'espace. Elle en est aujourd'hui une des adeptes les plus douées. Animée par une passion extrême pour l'approche qu'elle qualifie à la fois de classique et sophistiquée, Jennifer conçoit des décorations pures, caractérisées par leur fraîcheur et leur sobriété. Ses espaces ont converti même des traditionalistes au minimalisme. La lumière baigne chacun de ses cadres de vie, de sorte à les imprégner à la fois de sérénité et de chaleur, en juxtaposition cruciale avec la vie très active de ses clients. Des espaces caractérisés par de forts éléments architecturaux, des lignes sobres, des meubles sur mesure et des tons neutres ponctués par des touches de couleur dramatiques font la griffe très demandée de Jennifer Post. Une liste d'attente atteste d'un succès que Jennifer attribue à sa capacité d'écoute et donc de compréhension des goûts, souhaits et besoins de ses clients. Elle informe ceux qui souhaitent son look. Il s'agit d'une clientèle très sophistiquée. Jennifer, une femme d'affaires très dynamique avec l'âme d'une véritable artiste, entend susciter l'émerveillement de tous ceux qui ont fait l'expérience de ses intérieurs.

Jennifer Post, la arquitecta y diseñadora de interiores de Manhattan de fama internacional, ha formado parte durante décadas del movimiento moderno de diseño de espacios minimalistas pero elegantes, y es en la actualidad uno de los más talentosos devotos del género. Jennifer es extremadamente apasionada del enfoque que ella llama clásico y sofisticado y logra pureza de diseño a través de diseños simples y frescos. Sus espacios han logrado convertir en minimalistas aún a tradicionalistas. La luz inunda cada entorno, creando cualidades de serenidad y calidez, una yuxtaposición crucial para las complicadas vidas de sus clientes. Espacios que abarcan sólidos elementos arquitectónicos, líneas simples, mobiliario adaptado y tonos neutrales acentuados mediante colores dramáticos constituyen los elementos de alta demanda característicos de Jennifer Post. La lista de espera es testimonio del éxito que Jennifer considera producto de su capacidad para escuchar y, por lo tanto, reflejar los gustos, los deseos y las necesidades de sus clientes; educa a los que desean su estilo, sin duda una clientela muy sofisticada. Jennifer es una mujer de negocios de una enorme energía con el corazón de una artista de verdad, que aspira a provocar admiración en todas las personas que experimentan sus interiores.

Jennifer Post

NEW YORK

Above Left & Previous Page: I love to design in white. Its vibrancy and many interpretations stir the senses and lift the spirit. In a completely white space with illumination from all sources, no one element makes the room dramatic—it simply is. I designed the environment to encompass an Italian-made wall system with glass panels set into an aluminum frame and hung from ceiling tracks.

Above Right & Right: The apartment was just a concrete slab, a shell ... but it was an opportunity to discover the soul of the space. I came with a pad and began sketching. I believe architecture and furniture must speak the same language. The living room's 10-foot-long sofas and lean, ebonized low tables and the dining's high-gloss walnut-stained table are all arranged as architecture and strategically placed. For background color, the clients were looking forward to something a bit different than white. The furniture and the carpets are in soft blues, grays, beiges and olives. Real color was introduced through the art.

Facing Page: When my client purchased the loft, it was raw space: concrete floors and a single row of support columns. It had no plumbing, wiring or even wall partitions of any kind, but it did have 12-foot ceilings and 24 huge windows on four sides, with views of the Empire State Building and the New York skyline. Today, after two years of work, the 5,300-square-foot loft has eight rooms. To balance the great dimension of space, I commissioned several over-scaled pieces for the large rooms. I ordered a 12-foot-long custom sofa in soft purple wool and two extra-wide mustard-colored club chairs for the living area. The large art piece commands attention in brilliant red. Every room should have one strategically placed element of drama—big or small.

Photographs by Antoine Bootz

Above: I'm most definitely a perfectionist. When I feel an architectural element just belongs, I am hard pressed not to find a beautiful solution to the challenge my vision may present. I envisioned a staircase almost floating from the seventh floor to the eighth in a double-height space at the center of the residence. It was quite an engineering accomplishment to build it on-site, but we accomplished it through a lot of hard work. One of my proudest moments was learning I had been named to *Architectural Digest* AD Top 100. It reinforces that all the hard work, and the belief in one's own vision, really make an impression.

Facing Page Top: A wonderful example of my affinity for clean lines and aversion to curves: An expansive living/dining room on the main floor sets the tone for the rest of the Manhattan apartment. Dark walnut floors, white carpet and immaculate furnishings upholstered in white make a striking contrast. The long wall opposite the entrance is crafted of ebonized-white-oak panels flanking the limestone-clad fireplace. It's an incredibly functional storage area, which conceals a wine refrigerator in the dining area.

Facing Page Bottom: A stunning view of New York City complements the interior of a serene sitting room, which plays host to the famous skyline.
Photographs by Antoine Bootz

Top & Facing Page: I used a palette of white surfaces that seamlessly moves from matte to lacquer, from semi-gloss to high-gloss, from palest cream to softest pearl, from leather to limestone. The residents have an interesting art collection, notable for its inclusion of strong, pure colors, which I wanted to complement through light and furnishings. It was critical that the décor not overpower the art. While most of the furnishings are my signature white with clean straight lines, I added a few bold accent pieces that would echo the primary hues found in the art.

Bottom: We achieved flow throughout the large open spaces of a Tribeca apartment in the selection of materials including dark-stained woods and four types of limestone. Although the kitchen area is relatively small, it lives large.
Photographs by Antoine Bootz

"People confuse minimalism with cold, empty spaces. When done well, minimalist spaces are comfortable, engaging and very sophisticated."

—Jennifer Post

Marguerite Rodgers' spacious studio, a loft in the heart of Philadelphia's warehouse district, has a welcoming, warm, inspired ambience, much like that of the tailored interior environments she has been designing since founding her eponymous firm in 1980. Working alongside a team of 15 passionate interior designers and architects, Marguerite is recognized for her world-class interior designs that exhibit an attention to creative composition and meticulous detail. Her firm's custom spaces have an irresistibly serene and comfortable quality that invites life to be lived to its fullest. Possessing an artistic aptitude and flair for color, texture and materials the imaginative team is adept at the complete spectrum of design, from custom furniture to finishes and decorative details.

Le studio spacieux de Marguerite Rodgers, un loft au cœur du quartier des entrepôts de Philadelphie, est caractérisé par une ambiance chaleureuse, accueillante, inspirée, un peu comme celle des univers intérieurs sur mesure qu'elle conçoit depuis la fondation de la société qui porte son nom en 1980. Marguerite, qui travaille aux côtés d'une équipe de 15 décorateurs et architectes passionnés, est réputée pour ses décorations de niveau mondial qui témoignent d'un souci de la composition créative et du détail méticuleux. Les espaces personnalisés de sa société ont une qualité irrésistiblement sereine et confortable qui invite à vivre la vie au maximum. L'équipe créative est caractérisée par des aptitudes artistiques et un sens aigu de la couleur, de la texture et des matériaux, ainsi que son expertise dans le domaine du spectre complet de la conception, des meubles sur mesure à la finition et aux détails de décoration.

El espacioso estudio de Marguerite Rodgers, un loft en el corazón del distrito de almacenes de Filadelfia, presenta un ambiente acogedor, cálido e inspirado, que se asemeja a los entornos de interiores adaptados que ha venido diseñando desde la creación de la compañía que lleva su nombre en 1980. Trabajando junto a un equipo de 15 apasionados diseñadores de interiores y arquitectos, Marguerite es reconocida por sus diseños de interiores de nivel internacional, que exhiben una atención a la composición creativa y al detalle meticuloso. Los espacios personalizados de su compañía poseen una irresistible calidad serena y confortable que invita a vivir la vida con plenitud. Poseedores de una aptitud artística y un instinto por el color, la textura y los materiales, el imaginativo equipo es adepto al ciclo completo de diseño, desde los muebles personalizados hasta las terminaciones y detalles de decoración.

Marguerite V. Rodgers

PENNSYLVANIA

"A home must be warm, comfortable and livable."

—Marguerite V. Rodgers

Above: East Coast meets Far East, as the design pays homage to the home's locale and the residents' travels. The intriguing collection of oyster sticks, original George Nakashima furniture and rare Indonesian coffee table add authenticity to the great room. When the woven bamboo pocket door above the mantel is in the downward position, it reads as an architectural feature, completely concealing the television. I modeled the kitchen after the Japanese tansu with sliding cabinet doors to maximize the tight space.
Photograph by Barry Halkin

Facing Page Top: Because the residents wanted to be able to enjoy their retreat year-round, our design had to feel inviting on brisk wintery nights and refreshing on warm summer days. We kept the color palette soothingly neutral with natural red and green accents and incorporated Nakashima furniture and an exquisite antique rug.
Photograph by Matt Wargo

Facing Page Bottom: Guests delight in the inspiring aesthetic of the room, with the crisp linen sheets, vibrant red lacquer nightstand and thoughtful accents. I pulled the beautiful watercolors from an antique book and had them framed.
Photograph by Barry Halkin

Previous Page: The flat ceiling represents the original structure, but we expanded and enclosed the porch so that it could be more fully enjoyed. The high ceiling follows the roofline so it reads as a seamless addition from the outside and a spacious sanctuary inside. With an outdoor grill, sink, wet bar, granite counter and plenty of cabinet space, the area is used regularly. The horizontal paneling has a decidedly Japanese feel yet the detailing also nods to the Arts-and-Crafts period.
Photograph by Barry Halkin

Above: Without undertaking any architectural reorganization, we brought out the best in the suburban home by painting it a neutral palette and adding an eclectic array of art and objects. The varied materials and textures in the living room are fabulous—linen chairs, leather chairs, cotton sofa, bamboo table, sea-grass rug and stone fireplace, among others.
Photograph by Matt Wargo

Facing Page Top & Bottom: Nothing beats a true indoor-outdoor living scenario. Because of the home's prime location on the Chesapeake and the expansive views through the sliding glass wall systems, we didn't want the design to detract. We kept the colors and furnishings nature-inspired—the sea-foam green coverlet in the master bedroom, the earthy browns and beiges in the living room. Most of the furnishings throughout the home are modern—the leather Eames chairs, for example. The living room's table lamps, with their natural fiber shades, and floor lamp that has a glass dome top create an interesting geometry without departing too much from the clean lines.
Photographs by Barry Halkin

"Designs must first and foremost be appropriate—for the people as well as the location."

—Marguerite V. Rodgers

"As interior designers we listen well, imagine out loud and forge unforgettable, reflective spaces."
—Marguerite V. Rodgers

Top & Bottom: We love being able to create completely different aesthetics in people's primary and secondary residences. The powder room in New Jersey is completely tiled and exudes characteristics of a number of cultures, namely Spanish; the cabinet in the corner is filled with a collection of antique perfume bottles. As a dramatic counterpoint, the Pennsylvania condominium's foyer is the epitome of formal elegance. The walls and ceiling are stenciled with gold leafing; the floor, a handmade mosaic. We acquired antique Moroccan doors and fitted them perfectly into the space so they're authentically installed, without trim, on pivot hinges. To the right is a large closet; to the left is the powder room. Fortuny light fixtures, 18th-century Chinese sculptures and an antique Balinese chair round out the composition.

Facing Page Top: The upholstered bed sans skirt, Stark wool carpet with medium-scale pattern and defined seating area by the bay window culminate for a very tailored look. We have an art acquisitions department and worked with the homeowners to find the delicate oil paintings above the bed. It's really rewarding to work with people to build or round out their collections as their homes and needs evolve.

Facing Page Bottom: While the new homeowners were away on their honeymoon, we installed the furnishings and other decorative elements in the family room. I personally hung all of the round mirrors and wall calendars—and set them to the couple's wedding day—which create a definite focal point.
Photographs by Matt Wargo

Originally trained in architecture at Cornell University, José Solís instills a strong connection and respect for a space's existing context. Established structures and environments are never disregarded, but revered and incorporated to produce a seamless blend of old and new. José and his team of designers insist on making minute details feel appropriate to each project. Artwork and collections often serve as the driving force behind a design vision, adding a definitive and necessary texture to each space. Nearly two decades after founding Solis Betancourt, José works only with the most selective and established consultants and contractors to ensure each project achieves excellence.

José Solís, qui a étudié l'architecture à Cornell University, sait établir un lien solide avec le contexte existant, caractérisé par un profond respect pour celui-ci. Il ne néglige jamais les structures et les environnements avec lesquels il travaille. Au contraire, il leur rend hommage en les incorporant en mélange homogène d'ancien et de nouveau. José et son équipe de designers s'attachent à faire en sorte que les détails les plus infimes soient parfaitement adaptés à chaque projet. Des œuvres et collections d'art servent souvent d'inspiration à sa vision du design, et ajoutent une texture définitive et nécessaire à chaque espace. Près de vingt ans après avoir fondé Solis Betancourt, José ne travaille qu'avec les consultants et entrepreneurs les plus sélectifs et établis, de sorte à veiller à l'excellence de chaque projet.

Originalmente formado como arquitecto en la Universidad Cornell, José Solís transmite una sólida conexión y respeto por el contexto existente de un espacio. Las estructuras y entornos establecidos nunca se dejan de lado, son reverenciados e incorporados para producir una mezcla continua de lo viejo y lo nuevo. José y su equipo de diseñadores insisten en lograr que los detalles diminutos resulten apropiados para cada proyecto. A menudo las obras de arte y las colecciones sirven de fuerza propulsora detrás de una visión de diseño, agregando una textura definitiva y necesaria a cada espacio. Casi dos décadas después de fundar Solis Betancourt, José trabaja exclusivamente con los consultores y contratistas más selectivos y de mayor trayectoria para asegurarse de que cada proyecto logra la excelencia.

Solis Betancourt

WASHINGTON, D.C.

Above: Since the home is tucked away from the urban areas of Puerto Rico, we developed a farmhouse aesthetic for the interior. We felt very fortunate that the homeowners had an immense collection of Puerto Rican art, and we incorporated a ceramic piece by Jaime Suarez above the sofa. It is always exciting to mold a space around a particular piece of art and tailor the furnishings so that they don't overpower the room's centerpiece. Keeping with the relaxing atmosphere, a woven cane chair, mixed with cool blue linen fabrics, invokes a tropical experience.
Photograph by Gordon Beall

Facing Page: Dinner guests are sure to gather around the stunning art piece by Carter Potter whose technique—stretching camera film across canvas stretchers—captures the light to create an interesting luminosity. Upon close inspection, one can see the original images. Just beyond the dining room is the kitchen that evokes a rustic charm through its Moroccan tile backsplash, rustic beams, seeded glass French doors and pigmented plaster walls.
Photograph by Gordon Beall

Previous Page: The focus of the apartment was its panoramic views. We integrated both contemporary and traditional furnishings. An eclectic balance was achieved with sleek upholstered seating juxtaposing more traditional accent pieces. While the flooring and wall finish selections maintained a neutral palette, we added a dash of color via a gilded tea paper applied to the ceiling.
Photograph by Andrew Lautman

" Ivory is the new traditional palette. It enables clients to rotate artwork and give a fresh feeling to a space without the invasiveness of repainting the entire room."

—Paul Sherrill

Above: The dining room's verticality is one of its best assets—we worked with the double-height ceilings and draped fabrics harmoniously with the mid-century-style chandelier. A walnut table with a stretcher base and plank wood top serves more as an entry hall table for the family since most entertaining occurs outside. Anchoring the room is one of the client's favorite pieces of art: a large scale painting by José Morales.

Facing Page Top: Overlooking the generous lawn and golf course beyond, a modest bay seating area gives the study room a comfortable and leisurely ambience. Perhaps the most breathtaking piece within the room is the large painting by Epifanio Irizarry Jusino, which portrays traditional folk dancing in Puerto Rico. The family hosts dinners frequently and the artwork echoes the home's purpose: to entertain. On the coffee table we placed a rooster sculpture by Jorge Zeno; windows treatments of woven bamboo reflect the materials of the island.

Facing Page Bottom: A delicate color balance was achieved in the malt lavender guestroom. Here, an Irish wing chair in its original red silk velvet fabric was placed near a striking cerulean blue painting by Remigio Valdez. Modern vase sculptures contrast the richly encrusted nailhead Zanzibar chest to incorporate both contemporary and traditional elements.
Photographs by Gordon Beall

Top: A perfect niche contains a bed and night table set against a tobacco leaf wallcovering. Again, we wanted to keep the room neutral and used a light, natural linen to cover the headboard and included blue linen bolster and a whimsical basket-woven pillow.
Photograph by Gordon Beall

Bottom: Views overlooking the terrace and backyard add warmth to the interior colors and complement the vibrant bicycle rider painting by Arnaldo Roche. We looked to the artwork to inform our choice in rust-colored steamer club chairs and textured octagonal coffee table.
Photograph by Gordon Beall

Facing Page: My clients approached me desiring an apartment that exuded a traditional feel, but didn't mirror the accepted darkness among similar residences. To infuse this smaller space with light, we used ivory travertine floors with a golden mosaic border to reflect light. The library is articulated in cream painted woodwork and has frosted glass French doors in a contrasting dark walnut finish. Inviting guests as they enter is a Regency-inspired table accented with gilded details.
Photograph by John Hall

" All rooms should have individual, unique works of fine art. Without them a house lacks integrity."
—José Solís

For more than two decades Sroka Design has been designing extraordinary interior spaces of sophisticated elegance that harmoniously blend beauty with function. Principal Skip Sroka earned a degree in industrial design from the Cleveland Institute of Art before moving to Washington, D.C., in 1984. Skip is inspired by his travels and the perspective they bring to his work. He is also motivated by exquisite color combinations found throughout nature, which he often reinterprets to provide fresh, complementary colors to a room. Reading about and visiting historic sites completes his educated outlook. Sroka Design works in concert with architects from the earliest design stages: ensuring proportions are right for all living spaces, selecting materials, designing lighting plans, and creating cabinetry and mouldings. Skip creates engaging interior spaces that exude grace and sophistication yet are timeless and wonderfully livable.

Depuis plus de vingt ans, Sroka Design conçoit des espaces intérieurs extraordinaires par leur élégance sophistiquée qui associent harmonieusement beauté et fonctionnalité. Skip Sroka, son directeur, a obtenu son diplôme du Cleveland Institute of Art dans le domaine du dessin industriel avant de partir pour Washington en 1984. Skip s'inspire de ses voyages qui illuminent ses œuvres d'une perspective nouvelle. Il est également motivé par les exquises combinaisons de couleurs présentes dans toute la nature, qu'il réinterprète souvent pour agrémenter une pièce de couleurs fraîches et complémentaires. Des lectures au sujet de sites historiques et des visites de ceux-ci complètent sa vision éclairée. Sroka Design travaille en collaboration avec des architectes dès les premières phases de la conception : la société veille à l'adaptation des proportions à tous les espaces de séjour, à la sélection des matières, à la conception des plans d'éclairages, ainsi qu'à la création de pièces d'ébénisterie et de moulures. Skip crée des espaces intérieurs attrayants dont il émane un sentiment de grâce et de sophistication, mais qui restent intemporels et magnifiquement conviviaux.

Durante más de dos décadas, Sroka Design ha diseñado extraordinarios espacios interiores de una elegancia sofisticada, que combinan armoniosamente la belleza con la funcionalidad. Skip Sroka, su director, obtuvo su diploma de diseño industrial en el Instituto de Arte de Cleveland antes de mudarse a Washington, D.C., en 1984. Skip encuentra inspiración en sus viajes y la perspectiva que agregan a su trabajo. También lo motivan las exquisitas combinaciones de colores que se pueden encontrar en la naturaleza, a las que frecuentemente reinterpreta para brindar colores frescos y complementarios a una habitación. La visita a lugares históricos y la lectura sobre ellos completan su perspectiva educada. Sroka Design trabaja en conjunto con los arquitectos desde las primeras etapas de diseño: asegurándose de que las proporciones sean correctas para todos los espacios habitables, seleccionando materiales, diseñando planos de luces y creando gabinetes y molduras. Skip crea espacios interiores atractivos que exudan gracia y sofisticación y, al mismo tiempo, resultan atemporales y maravillosamente habitables.

Skip Sroka

MARYLAND

Above: The intimate sitting room beckons you to enjoy it alone or with friends. Velvet mohair covers one of the sofas. Woven shades permit just the right amount of light. The coffee table features a limestone top whose smooth texture lends to the tactile diversity of the space.

Right: Lacking the perfect piece of furniture that would convey the strength needed for the foyer, I designed an ideal console to fit, which is comprised of walnut, ebony and anigre in the center panel. Handcrafted artisan glass complements the piece. The mirror above picks up the ebony of the console and reflects the handpainted design between mouldings, which help to create a more human scale to a room with considerable ceiling height.

Facing Page: Art acquired from Stephen Haller Gallery in New York is center stage in the chic dining room. Deep brown walls, a light blue ceiling and soft lighting create an ideal backdrop for the extraordinary piece. A circular motif begins with the grand lighting fixture, which features a mica shade. The shape is mirrored through a large bowl centered on the table as well as in the mullions of the cabinetry. The supple leather chairs contrast with a textured wool carpet.

Previous Page: In the corner of a relaxed family room, curvilinear elements play against squared shapes. A striking blue bowl found at the Baltimore Craft Show, the round coffee table, spherical forms in the lamp, rounded features in the bookcases and curved-back dining chairs create their own sense of balance and take the edge off what could otherwise have been a very linear space.

Photographs by Timothy Bell

Above: Everyone who enters the elegant dining room cannot help but feel chic. The studs in the drapery treatments also appear in the leather border of the rug. Despite the continental Italian console and the crystal and silver chandelier, the room is anything but stuffy. Tasteful, Deco-inspired chairs upholstered in woven chenille complement the composition.

Facing Page: French doors invite passage into the relaxing bathroom where the ceiling over the tub forms a three-dimensional arch over the window. Horizontal sheers cover the doors, providing privacy in a space suited for leisure. The chair is upholstered in a Sunbrella terry cloth fabric so one can sit down right out of the tub without a care in the world. Floor patterns are subtle, enhancing the sense of space.
Photographs by Timothy Bell

Top: The room is elegant and understated at the same time. Rug corners step out of the squared design to accentuate the perfect square shape of the room. A circle of studs in the rug echoes the round table, which I designed expressly for this space, helping to create harmony. The owners love the way the light fills the room and creates a soft, airy ambience.

Bottom: In the gracious entry foyer, floors inlaid with limestone connect with columns to create a compelling geometric grid. The great goat leg table with overscale lantern has strong graphic presence. The seven-foot-tall mirror reflects light streaming across a staircase on the opposite side of the room—the space is handsome and refined.

Facing Page: A narrow outdoor room in an urban setting, the screened-in porch is enjoyed year-round by the homeowners. The drapery allows light to filter throughout the space while preserving valuable privacy. Water-resistant materials enable everything to remain carefree.
Photographs by Timothy Bell

From her nursery school days, toddling through New York museums, to her education at both Yale and Columbia Universities, Lisa Adams' life has all the right ingredients for a beaming interior design career. An intuitive vision for spacing, lines and color is paired with her vast business and finance knowledge, allowing Lisa's clients to rest securely in impeccable results that honor their parameters. Never embracing a signature style, Lisa discovers the intricacies of each homeowner, which undoubtedly assists in the development of both large and small details in a home. With a gentle mixture of antiques, these interesting elements add history, ornament and complexity to Lisa's forward-thinking designs.

De sa plus tendre enfance à son éducation aux universités de Yale et Columbia, en passant par ses visites aux musées de New York alors qu'elle n'était qu'une petite fille, la vie de Lisa Adams comporte tous les ingrédients nécessaires à une brillante carrière dans le domaine de la décoration intérieure. Elle associe une vision intuitive de l'espacement, des lignes et des couleurs à de vastes connaissances dans le domaine des affaires et des finances, de sorte que les clients de Lisa savent qu'ils peuvent compter sur des résultats impeccables qui font honneur à leurs paramètres. Lisa n'adopte jamais un style particulier, et met en lumière les subtilités de la personnalité de chaque propriétaire, ce qui facilite sans nul doute le choix des petits et grands détails d'une maison. Associés à un mélange subtil d'antiquités, ces éléments apportent histoire, ornementation et complexité aux créations innovantes de Lisa.

Desde sus años en la guardería infantil, paseando por los museos de Nueva York, hasta su paso por las universidades de Yale y Columbia, la vida de Lisa Adams incluye todos los ingredientes para una maravillosa carrera en diseño de interiores. Una visión intuitiva del espacio, las líneas y el color se complementa con su enorme entusiasmo y profundo conocimiento de finanzas que permite a sus clientes estar seguros de obtener resultados impecables que honrarán sus parámetros. Sin concentrarse en un estilo característico, Lisa descubre las intrincadas particulares de cada propietario, lo que sin duda contribuye al proceso de desarrollo de pequeños y grandes detalles en un hogar. Mediante una delicada combinación de antigüedades, tales elementos interesantes agregan historia, ornamento y complejidad sus diseños de avanzada.

Lisa Adams

WASHINGTON, D.C.

Above: The goal of the master bedroom was to keep it very simple and clean. The home is perched on a mountain in Alabama, and I wanted the space to have strong character pulled from its furniture and natural views. To give my client an access space in the room, I placed two chairs in front of the textural concrete fireplace.
Photograph by Alan Dynerman

Facing Page: While most bathrooms are narrow and push all the furniture against the walls, I took the opportunity to use a plentiful room to approach this bathing space differently. The dominant element in the room is an island sink that's actually designed for kitchen use—I placed a double-sided hanging mirror from one of the pot racks, which allows the homeowners to use the piece from all sides. As is typical with European styles, the shower has no partitions and the water flows to a drain beneath the teak flooring.
Photograph by Lydia Cutter

Previous Page: Designed with a distinct contemporary flair, the living room functions well for both formal and informal gatherings of all sizes. Great architectural features—such as the wood-slats across the window—made the space a pleasure to design. The home is located high on a mountain in Alabama and receives a generous amount of light, so I chose to use an accent wall in an ochre earth tone. Layering the house from the bottom to the top with color, I designed custom rugs to provide additional texture and pattern and complement the lighter seating pieces.
Photograph by Alan Dynerman

"Beautiful landscapes should not be obscured by the design—they should be integral to it."

—Lisa Adams

Top: Overlooking the front of the house, the space needed some definition. I incorporated function into the second-floor landing by designing a window seat for my clients, who are avid readers. Now the homeowners can read, sit or comfortably look out the window, because I turned the empty transition space into a destination all its own.

Bottom: My approach to a powder room is simple: since it's not a place where homeowners usually spend a large amount of time, it should be as entertaining as possible for guests. I took an old reproduction credenza and turned it into a dramatic vanity by placing a brass sink in the center. The space was kept very clean but interesting with book-print wallpaper, leather-bound books, tortoise shell pieces and dark wood.

Facing Page: The room has a bright bedspread, a dramatic tray ceiling, an inviting fireplace and a beautiful interplay of subtle textural and fabric patterns. The bed is set high enough that the homeowners can look out onto blooming fruit trees and the expansive landscape. By keeping the palette neutral, I allowed the room's natural setting to blend seamlessly with the room's décor.
Photographs by Peter Leach

"Rooms should be simple with clean lines—forms speak for themselves without embellishment."

—Lisa Adams

More than two decades ago, Pat Bibbee began laying the foundation for a higher approach to interior design in West Virginia. At the center of her philosophy is a deep and often lifelong, investment in clients' interests, needs and goals. Whether doling out design advice during the construction phase or offering a guiding voice through the plethora of interior options, Pat is dedicated to superior design solutions, which has established her as a trusted and distinguished designer across the country. In addition to creating new spaces, Pat interacts with the West Virginia Governor's Mansion Preservation Committee and other historical renovations, contributing to a balanced yet exciting interior design style.

Il y a plus de 20 ans, Pat Bibbee a commencé à poser les fondations d'une approche plus sophistiquée de l'architecture intérieure en Virginie de l'Ouest. Au centre de sa philosophie se trouve un investissement profond et souvent pour la vie entière en faveur de la défense des intérêts du client, de ses besoins et objectifs. Qu'elle offre des conseils en matière de design au cours de la phase de construction ou qu'elle guide les clients au sein d'une pléthore d'options, Pat s'engage à offrir des solutions au plus haut niveau en matière de design, qui lui ont permis de s'imposer dans l'ensemble du pays comme une architecte distinguée et digne de confiance. Pat ne se contente pas de créer de nouveaux espaces, elle travaille en collaboration avec le comité pour la préservation du manoir du Gouverneur de la Virginie de l'Ouest et participe à d'autres travaux de rénovation historique, contribuant à un style d'architecture intérieure à la fois équilibré et passionnant.

Más de dos décadas atrás, Pat Bibbee comenzó a construir las bases de un enfoque superior al diseño de interiores en Virginia Occidental. En el centro de su filosofía se encuentra una profunda y frecuentemente de por vida dedicación a los intereses, necesidades y objetivos de sus clientes. Ya sea prodigando consejos sobre diseño durante la fase de construcción u ofreciendo un guía a través de la profusión de opciones de interiores, Pat tiene un compromiso con las soluciones de diseño superiores, que la ha establecido como una diseñadora confiable y distinguida en todo el país. Además de la creación de nuevos espacios, Pat interactúa con el Comité de Preservación de la Mansión del Gobernador de Virginia Occidental y otras renovaciones históricas, contribuyendo a un estilo de diseño de interiores balanceado y excitante a la vez.

Pat Bibbee

Above Left: After living in the house for quite some time with a living room that consisted of a Chippendale sofa and uninviting Martha Washington chairs, the owners needed to turn their space into a warm and welcoming room. Inspired by an Oriental rug in another part of the house, I chose a classic Tiffany's shade of aqua for the room, perfectly complementing the couple's extensive monogrammed silver collection.

Above Right: Mixing fabrics is often a delicate art to balance, but in the rustic dining room—which opens out to a courtyard garden—and adjacent sitting room, deep blue and white patterns come together seamlessly.

Right: Quiet colors were chosen to yield to the breathtaking views of West Virginia's capitol. Every room in the three-story house on the Kanawha River overlooks this very spot, and at night the surroundings are brilliantly displayed and never have to compete with the interior.

Facing Page: When The Greenbrier was being renovated, I purchased these Dorothy Draper dining room chairs and recovered them in a pink velvet fabric to make a perfect addition to the dark table. The bold pink color statement makes the room dramatic and glamorous. The chandelier is original to the 1936 house.

Previous Page: For a cottage at The Greenbrier, the homeowner wanted bright colors but still a more traditional ambience. Upbeat fabrics such as aqua and polka dot paired with other coral and neutral hues give the space a subtle contemporary flair.
Photographs by John Smith

"Within a home, one should be drawn from room to room with a subtle memory of what's been left behind. Rooms should fall into one another."

—Pat Bibbee

Top: Offering an elegant retreat to visitors, the guestroom is delicately dressed in toile fabrics and aqua-striped wallpaper.

Bottom: An antique loveseat recovered in a yellow Chinese fabric offers a simple yet inviting presence to the entryway of the home.

Facing Page Top: West Virginia has some of the most gorgeous nature and in an addition, the kitchen and family room were dressed in soft blue and cream tones. To give the area a dimensional quality and complete the homeowners' art collection, we placed some sculptural plates along the wall.

Facing Page Bottom: Within the house's back entry, a contemporary fabric covers a traditional chair and serves as a stronger continuation of other blue tones in the home.
Photographs by John Smith

The world is Geoffrey Bradfield's canvas. Drawing inspiration from the uniqueness of the Orient, African Primitivism and Art Deco, among other niche genres, Geoffrey savors the opportunity to incorporate fine art and rare antiques into his clients' lives. Though he founded his namesake firm, Geoffrey Bradfield Inc., in the early '90s, the designer has been practicing his life's passion for upward of four decades and has somehow managed to make each commission even more spectacular than the last. Whether designing within a sleek loft, palatial estate, period bungalow, jet plane or private yacht, the South African-born, New York-based designer infuses his work with an internationally inspired, timelessly modern aesthetic—and if a design warrants, a piece or two from his stunning Millennium Modern Lucite furniture line or his Stark Carpet Signature Collection. Each of Geoffrey's designs is freshly tailored, yet all exude a certain functional opulence that nods at once to the past, present and future.

Le monde est la toile de Geoffrey Bradfield. Geoffrey, qui tire son inspiration du caractère unique de l'Orient, du Primitivisme africain et de l'Art Déco entre autres genres particuliers, savoure l'opportunité d'incorporer les beaux-arts et les antiquités rares à la vie de ses clients. Même s'il a fondé la société qui porte son nom, Geoffrey Bradfield Inc., au début des années 90, le designer s'adonne à la passion de sa vie depuis plus de quarante ans et est parvenu à faire en sorte que chaque commission soit encore plus spectaculaire que la précédente. Qu'il s'agisse de l'aménagement d'un loft sophistiqué, du domaine d'un palais, d'un bungalow historique, d'un avion ou d'un yacht privé, le designer new-yorkais originaire d'Afrique du Sud infuse son travail d'une esthétique moderne et intemporelle d'inspiration internationale, et si un design l'exige, d'une pièce ou deux des meubles de sa fantastique collection Millennium Modern Lucite ou de sa collection de tapis Stark. Chacune des œuvres de Geoffrey est simplement conçue, mais il en émane une certaine opulence fonctionnelle évocatrice à la fois du passé, du présent et de l'avenir.

El mundo es el lienzo de Geoffrey Bradfield. Inspirándose en la singularidad del Oriente, el primitivismo africano y el estilo Art Deco, entre otros géneros de nicho, Geoffrey se deleita de la oportunidad de incorporar obras de arte y antigüedades excepcionales a las vidas de sus clientes. A pesar de haber fundado la compañía que lleva su nombre, Geoffrey Bradfield Inc., a principios de la década del 90, el diseñador ha practicado la pasión de su vida por más de cuatro décadas y de alguna manera ha logrado que cada comisión resulte más espectacular que la anterior. Ya sea diseñando dentro de un loft estilizado, una propiedad palaciega, un bungalow de época, un avión a reacción o un yate privado, el diseñador de origen sudafricano con sede en Nueva York infunde a su obra una estética de modernidad clásica de inspiración internacional y, si el diseño lo amerita, una pieza o dos de su magnífica línea de mobiliario moderno de lucita Millennium o de su colección de alfombras Stark Signature. Cada uno de los diseños de Geoffrey es personalizado y, sin embargo, todos ellos destilan una cierta opulencia funcional con detalles simultáneos del pasado, presente y futuro.

Geoffrey Bradfield

NEW YORK ■ FLORIDA ■ DUBAI

Above: I've reinterpreted the Art Deco period for today's lifestyle, drawing inspiration from RKO films and the escapist fantasies that took viewers' breath away with their sleek, sinuous scenery and precise chorus lines of leggy, lissome Follies Girls. The library's cocoon-like ambience and captivating textures and contrast are achieved through the brilliant combination of fine art, sumptuous copper taffeta draperies, raw burlap wallcovering and exotic Macassar ebony furnishings upholstered in burnt apricot. The homeowner and I jaunted to Paris to acquire Art Deco antiques for his Palm Beach residence. What we couldn't find, I designed and had fabricated in France—the gondola-style chair was created from my exacting specifications. The classic nude by Renneson, 1921 Albert Gleizes *Composition à Deux Personnages* and 1930s' hand-blown French vase are essential to the space's composition.

Facing Page: I encourage clients to invest in the finest art and furnishings they can afford. Since the homeowner acquired the Art Deco chest of drawers with ivory inlay, its value has more than quadrupled. The bedroom's luxurious striae walls provide a calming backdrop for the bronze *Femme Nu aux Bras Levés* by Csaky and organically abstract painting by South American artist Roberto Matta, which the 1930s' mirror beautifully restates.

Previous Page: Reinventing the Palm Beach residence's architectural elements was the first step in transforming it into a chic Art Deco haven with 21st-century perspective. The house was designed around a courtyard, and I maximized the views and enhanced the indoor-outdoor connectivity by replacing a series of standard-sized doors and windows with floor-to-ceiling panes of glass. Both the living room and its poolside backdrop are informed by masterful balance and symmetry: chairs custom fabricated in Paris; clean-lined columns; centrally positioned pool, Stark carpet and table; fireplace on the north wall and monumental sculpture directly south. The 3,200-pound Enrique Mancini head—situated in front of a black mirror—appears to float above the jet-black pool, which I completely redesigned to transcend mere leisure and function as an aesthetically interesting element to enjoy rain or shine.
Photographs by Kim Sargent

"No decade of the 20th century had such a distinctive flavor and legendary atmosphere as the '20s. One cannot underestimate the impact of the Art Deco period on our lifestyle and in how we perceive our interiors today."

—Geoffrey Bradfield

Top: Setting the ambience and style at point of entry is imperative. The Art Deco theme sets a tone of welcome with Simonet Frères sconces, which complement the cascading natural light; large-scale gilt mirror; and sculptural marble and wrought iron Gilbert Poillerat console tables. The balanced yet interesting lines of the consoles, their symmetrical placement within the space and the manner in which they are reflected further nod to the Art Deco styling.

Bottom: The harmonious interplay of texture, contrast and color lends comfortable opulence to the living room. Drawing inspiration from Rulhman's period textiles, I designed the sofa as well as the silk and wool rug, which embodies the essence of the jazz age and enlivens the space with bold and somewhat unexpected lines. I also designed the Art Deco-style dental-inlaid commode, which offsets the Dupagne cloaked figure. To exaggerate the height of the 10-foot ceilings, I specified Brunschwig & Fils draperies—ivory silk, lined with Tudor-red taffeta—that deliberately meet the floor in an extravagant puddle. In addition to providing a punch of color to the soothing palette, the contemporary window treatment appropriately frames the courtyard's central figure: the Mancini head.

Facing Page Top: Like a Fabergé egg, the dining room envelops guests with its pristine yet comfortable ambience. The reflective wall invites the lushly landscaped formal courtyard indoors while limestone flooring and diamond-studded wallpaper provide a refined, neutral backdrop for the rich combination of antique and custom furnishings. The circa-1925 French chandelier, acquired from Sotheby's, is a clever counterpoint to the 1970s' Lichtenstein relief that hangs on the mirrored surface. Beige mohair chairs surround the pedestal table with vegetable ivory inlay. Because each detail has been concisely edited, the space feels at once luxurious and finely appointed.

Facing Page Bottom: It's easy to envision the likes of Ava Gardner descending the staircase—the Macassar ebony and brushed steel create an intriguing, Old Hollywood sophistication. While the original stairway spiraled down awkwardly in the center of the room, the new interpretation blends harmoniously and makes great use of the space. The organic form of Lambert-Rucki's minstrels sculpture visually balances the stairs and emphasizes the room's pleasing geometry. When thoughtfully selected, art can add a new dimension of uniqueness to any space. Art makes environments personal; it makes them come to life. The bronze Lambert-Rucki at the foot of the staircase, stacked stone Boaz Vaadia figure on the coffee table and marble Mancini head beyond the glass—among others—can be enjoyed from a variety of perspectives in the living room and adjacent spaces.

Photographs by Kim Sargent

" Even asymmetrical compositions, ideally, should achieve symmetry."
—Geoffrey Bradfield

Design visions have been a way of life for Arlene Critzos. Having lived and studied internationally, decorative arts and interior design became her passion. When Arlene founded Interior Concepts in 1979 she quickly realized that by broadening the design capabilities of her company she and her staff could work in multiple creative paths. The firm has a staff of 80 people divided into design divisions from high-end residential to commercial. The design divisions allow Arlene and her highly talented and tenured senior design group to create and complete work in the most professional manner. Arlene and Interior Concepts have worked in England, Spain, the Middle East, Malaysia, China and the United States.

Arlene Critzos vit dans un monde de visions créatives. Elle a vécu et étudié dans différents pays, et les arts décoratifs et la décoration intérieure sont sa passion. Lorsque Arlene a fondé Interior Concepts en 1979, elle a vite compris qu'en élargissant les capacités d'invention de la société, elle et son personnel pourraient emprunter de multiples chemins créatifs. La société emploie 80 personnes réparties en divisions, du résidentiel de haut de gamme au commercial. Les divisions consacrées à la décoration permettent à Arlene et à son groupe permanent expérimenté et de grand talent de créer et de réaliser des travaux de la manière la plus professionnelle. Arlene et Interior Concepts ont travaillé en Angleterre, en Espagne, dans le Moyen-Orient, en Malaisie, en Chine et aux États-Unis.

Las visiones de diseño han sido una forma de vida para Arlene Critzos. Habiendo vivido y estudiado internacionalmente, las artes decorativas y el diseño de interiores se convirtieron en su pasión. Cuando Arlene fundó Interior Concepts en 1979, se dio cuenta rápidamente de que ampliando las capacidades de diseño de la compañía, tanto ella como su personal podrían trabajar en múltiples áreas de diseño. La compañía tiene un plantel de 80 personas repartidas en divisiones de diseño, desde el área residencial de lujo hasta la comercial. Las divisiones de diseño permiten a Arlene y a su muy talentoso y experimentado grupo de diseño senior crear y terminar obras de una manera extremadamente profesional. Arlene e Interior Concepts han trabajado en Inglaterra, España, Medio Oriente, Malasia, China y los Estados Unidos.

Arlene Critzos

Above & Previous Page: Within a home that is truly European eclectic, the design of massive 12-by-14-foot antique doors from a château in France dictated the scale of the room. Massive gothic windows, oversized draperies and the sculpture of David are all in balance of the doors. From contemporary to French to Asian and Italian, the styles are a great mix of inclusive aesthetics. A powerful painting of a monk with child from the Murillo school centers the main living space. The two-story gothic windows join up with a classical European mix of furniture.

Left: A cozy family room vignette comes across as transitional, with clean lines. The linen gauze draperies filter light to the paisley cashmere chairs.

Facing Page Top: The homeowner wanted a very casual, coastal-inspired interior, seen in the conversation and viewing area of a great room on Figure Eight Island. The clean, streamlined look matches the powerful interior architecture. With off-white walls, bone-textured chairs and a coconut-shell cocktail table, the room reflects the natural habitat outside the large windows.

Facing Page Bottom: Chocolate walls meet crisp white trim and lush Italian bedding. The headboard is a twist on a classical motif. The Sumac rug anchors the room.
Photographs by Gordon Beall

"My style, in general, is gathered, rather than pure. There are more surprises that way."

—Arlene Critzos

Top: Leading to an outdoor living area, the cozy sitting area is stimulated by a magnificent wall fresco. The historic reference is from Salzburg's famous Pferdeschwemme, where large panels of magnificent horses adorn the outdoor square—the archbishop's horses were bathed there. The handmade chair and table are made of twigs and stems.

Bottom: The perfect geometry of a clean-lined Italianate loggia comes about in the residence. Each quadrant is perfectly balanced by stone-floor and plaster-ceiling details—a natural stage for an 18th-century French horse art collection, an exquisite console of 18th-century Boulle and sculpture.

Facing Page Top: The 18th-century English Parlor exudes power in color and style. The Georgian mouldings and details throughout dictated the classicism required. The client's love of strong color—yellows, whites, golds and cherry red—along with refined antiques from around the world brought the residence to perfection.

Facing Page Bottom: The twist shows clearly in the rich and diverse room. Eggplant-colored walls work as an envelope to all soft-textured neutrals. A Dutch marquetry headboard juxtaposes with clean-lined linens and chairs. A statement mirror moves the wall and reflects the entire space.
Photographs by Gordon Beall

Whether a home is in the conceptualization phase or its final accessories are being placed on a library shelf, Patricia Gorman loves the process of producing cohesive palettes of eclectic styles. And if she's not rejuvenating her design inspirations at a family home on the eastern shore, then she's most likely wrapped up in the latest bedtime story with her grandchildren. A boundless energy and love of challenges serve as the perfect match to her natural inquisitiveness when traveling through local antique and flea markets around the world. As the principal of Patricia Gorman Associates, Patricia uses unique international styles to constantly challenge, influence and refresh her perspectives. By integrating her clients' desires into fresh designs, Patricia consistently finds a way to reflect the homeowners' heart and soul in every project.

Qu'il s'agisse de la phase de conceptualisation d'une maison ou que l'on dispose des accessoires sur les étagères d'une bibliothèque, Patricia Gorman est passionnée par le processus de production de palettes cohérentes de styles éclectiques. Lorsqu'elle ne régénère pas ses inspirations en matière de décoration dans une maison familiale sur la Côte Est, elle est probablement immergée dans la dernière histoire de chevet qu'elle lit à ses petits-enfants. Une énergie illimitée et une passion pour les défis complètent parfaitement sa curiosité naturelle lorsqu'elle visite les magasins locaux d'antiquités et les marchés aux puces du monde entier. À la tête de Patricia Gorman Associates, Patricia se sert de styles internationaux uniques pour constamment remettre en question, influencer et rafraîchir ses perspectives. Elle incorpore les souhaits de ses clients pour proposer des décorations intérieures innovantes. Elle trouve constamment de nouvelles manières de faire en sorte que chaque projet soit le reflet du cœur et de l'âme du propriétaire de la maison.

Independientemente de si un hogar se encuentra en la fase de conceptualización o de si se están colocando los accesorios en un estante de la biblioteca, Patricia Gorman adora el proceso de producción de catálogos cohesivos de estilos eclécticos. Si no está rejuveneciendo sus inspiraciones de diseño en un hogar de familia de la Costa Este, muy probablemente se encuentre muy ocupada leyendo un cuento a sus nietos antes de dormir. Una energía sin límites y una pasión por los desafíos sirven como complemento perfecto a su curiosidad natural cuando visita mercados de antigüedades y de pulgas en todo el mundo. Como directora de Patricia Gorman Associates, Patricia utiliza estilos internaciones exclusivos para desafiar, influenciar y rejuvenecer constantemente sus perspectivas. Mediante la integración de los deseos de sus clientes a diseños nuevos, Patricia consistentemente encuentra la manera de reflejar el corazón y el alma de los propietarios en cada proyecto.

Patricia Gorman

Above: A classical Georgian brick home in the Philadelphia suburbs has a delicate balance of traditional furnishings and contemporary art. The marble fireplace and millwork with a coffered ceiling make the area a comfortable place for entertaining.
Photograph by Matt Wargo

Right: The absence of fluff in coordination with a straightforward style invokes an inviting atmosphere within the great room of a Colorado home. An Arts-and-Crafts style is complemented by a warm blend of wood, iron and stonework.
Photograph by David Marlow

Facing Page: With her main residence in New York and the secondary home located in Colorado, my client wasn't looking for a home that echoed a traditional mountain style. We were fortunate to have a raw space and reworked the floorplan to accommodate a vaulted ceiling with a truss and beam structure. By rearranging rooms, we changed the space completely and gave it a lofty feel. Items from the client's impressive art and photography collection fill the house, including a triptych of cloud formations near the dining area.
Photograph by David Marlow

Previous Page: Sitting as an impressive piece in the living room is a large, hand-chiseled limestone fireplace; its elevation was designed so that it can be seen from both sides of the great room and an adjacent sitting room. Mixing antiques with Old World furnishings, I achieved the client's goal: to have a romantic space—that is both timeless and comfortable—that feels as if it has been lived in for quite some time. Adding to the ambience are plaster walls and a custom chandelier whose handpainted scene is reminiscent of the Colorado mountainside.
Photograph by David Marlow

Top: To provide my client with a divided privacy space off her master bedroom, I designed a semi-circular moveable wall panel system made out of iron and a luminescent resin product. The grid is circular, allowing the panels to stack up against one another and open the space completely. Since the home has a distinct contemporary ambience, I used concrete floors and elongated the firebox by placing burning candles to the left of the fireplace.
Photograph by David Marlow

Bottom: The vanity in the guest bathroom uses pleasant, sandblasted, frosted glass. Counter space was doubled by choosing a raised countertop sink—guests cannot only admire the volume of the sink, but they also have a recessed space for storage.
Photograph by David Marlow

Facing Page: For an active family with small children, the kitchen's layout needed to facilitate flexible cooking and cleanup processes within an engaging environment. I chose a stunning German silver sink with a custom-designed circuitous dividing line, a warm butter color and a French tin countertop with a rolled edge on the island. To offset the cabinetry and give a continuous glow from the tin and stainless steel, I incorporated a backsplash comprised of beautiful metallic tiles.
Photograph by Matt Wargo

"This is the beauty of design: we deliver the imaginable."
—Patricia Gorman

For years Maureen Griffin Balsbaugh was in clothing design. When she made the transition to interior design more than a decade ago, she found a new level of satisfaction, for the homeowner's response to the project is perceptible. With Griffin Balsbaugh Interiors, Maureen finds herself transforming spaces—from modern to traditional—all over New England. There is no true niche in her work; Maureen gets the feel for the project by becoming part of the family, discovering the client's personal style. That and a long history of skilled work make for a wonderfully unique project each time.

Maureen Griffin Balsbaugh a travaillé pendant des années dans le domaine de la création de mode. Lorsqu'elle est passée à la décoration intérieure il y a plus de dix ans, elle y a trouvé de nouvelles satisfactions, dans la mesure où la réaction du propriétaire de la maison était perceptible. Au sein de Griffin Balsbaugh Interiors, Maureen peut transformer des espaces, du moderne au traditionnel, dans toute la Nouvelle Angleterre. Son travail ne correspond à aucun véritable créneau particulier. Maureen acquiert une compréhension intuitive du projet en s'intégrant à la famille, en découvrant le style personnel du client. Ainsi, et en s'appuyant sur sa longue expérience de ce travail spécialisé, elle réalise à chaque fois un projet magnifiquement unique.

Durante muchos años, Maureen Griffin Balsbaugh se dedicó al diseño de ropa. Cuando llevó a cabo la transición al diseño de interiores, hace más de una década, encontró un nuevo nivel de satisfacción en el que la respuesta del propietario al proyecto resulta perceptible. Con Griffin Balsbaugh Interiors, Maureen se dedica a transformar espacios modernos y tradicionales en toda Nueva Inglaterra. No existe un nicho para su trabajo; Maureen se familiariza con el proyecto convirtiéndose en parte de la familia, descubriendo el estilo personal del cliente. Todo lo anterior y un amplio historial de trabajo experto dan como resultado un proyecto maravillosamente exclusivo en cada oportunidad.

Maureen Griffin Balsbaugh

MASSACHUSETTS

Above: A one-car garage in Nantucket often goes unused. I transformed the space into a media room, sueded the walls, and basically built a cocoon to curl into for those rainy, foggy New England days.

Facing Page Top: The architecture of the room was so well done that laying out the furniture was a somewhat simple task. The central mirror and fireplace are great matches for the oval windows.

Facing Page Bottom: The 270-year-old home needed to be entirely rehabbed. The room is very light, very bright, and so I never forced anything, as that would have thrown the scale. I had the chairs upholstered in a cutup rug for the fascinating pattern.

Previous Page: The homeowner loved blue. Designing furniture and fabrics for the formal dining room was a great opportunity to age the new home so that it transcends time. The rich texture flows with the desired color palette to create a very comfortable, very serene space.
Photographs by Sam Gray

"Scale is the most important thing in design."
—Maureen Griffin Balsbaugh

Top: The Nantucket media room needed the perfect sofa to curl into on bad weather days. I designed the piece to be high in the back and very deep—and to stretch the whole length of the room to fit several people if need be.

Bottom: The home was a bit upside down in structure, with a spiral stair right up the middle. I wanted to frame the ocean views, so I chose a sea glass palette: pale blues, greens—soothing colors that are very relaxing.

Facing Page: A Juarez Machado painting is the focal point of the 14-foot room. High drapes really accent the room's scale. A link to the painting's red dress is the 16th-century Italian chair, which has the original upholstering. Taupes, reds, creams and browns: The color palette is smooth and inviting.
Photographs by Sam Gray

Located in the heart of Princeton, Judy King Interiors is part antique shop, part design studio. For Judy King, a vast collection of European textiles in tandem with a large design library is an important foundation. Here she combines French and English 19th-century antiques and reproductions with a love of discovering new ways to express color and fabric. The daughter of an interior designer, Judy has spent a lifetime studying the spaces in which we live. With many publications behind her, including a recent cover of *NY Spaces*, Judy looks for the personal and the unique in each of her projects.

Situé au cœur de Princeton, Judy King Interiors est à la fois un magasin d'antiquités et un studio de création. Judy King voit dans une vaste collection de textiles européens associée à une large bibliothèque de dessins une fondation importante de son travail. Elle associe des antiquités françaises et anglaises du 19e siècle et des reproductions de celles-ci à une passion pour la découverte de nouvelles façons d'exprimer la couleur et la texture. Judy est la fille d'une décoratrice et a consacré sa vie à l'étude des espaces dans lesquels nous vivons. Elle a fait l'objet de nombreuses publications, en particulier une couverture récente de NY Spaces, et s'attache toujours aux aspects personnels et uniques de chacun de ses projets.

Ubicado en el corazón de Princeton, Judy King Interiors es en parte una tienda de antigüedades y en parte un estudio de diseño. Para Judy King, una vasta colección de textiles europeos junto a un amplio catálogo de diseño constituye una base sólida. Judy combina antigüedades y reproducciones francesas e inglesas del siglo XIX con una pasión por el descubrimiento de nuevas maneras de expresar el color y las telas. Judy, hija de un diseñador de interiores, dedicó toda su vida al estudio de los espacios en los que vivimos. Con diversas publicaciones en su haber, incluyendo una tapa reciente de la revista NY Spaces, Judy constantemente busca lo personal y exclusivo en cada uno de sus proyectos.

Judy King

NEW JERSEY

Above Left & Right: We really shot for neutral. The Chinese elm flooring pairs nicely with Holly Hunt pendants, rattan chairs and a thick concrete slab for the kitchen countertop. The door was reclaimed from a cruise ship, and color was brought in with the red window treatment and back wall.
Photograph by Tom Grimes

Facing Page Top: The homeowner is an entrepreneur who works from home, so we transformed his living room to coincide with an office. Terracotta walls and a zebra ottoman give an earthy flavor, while the Asian blue daybed brings in a great splash of color.
Photograph by Tom Grimes

Facing Page Bottom: The client has two loves: yoga and entertaining. Materials reclaimed from an old barn found new life as a yoga studio, with heated concrete floors, high ceilings and a Buddha head to find Zen-like qualities. Open the curtains and a great entertaining space reveals itself.
Photograph by Tom Grimes

Previous Page: A gentleman's library begs to have a cigar smoked inside; the room exhibits masculinity with dark woods, a hidden liquor room, leather and trophies—a veritable clubroom for the budding Hemmingway.
Photograph by Peter Rymwid

"The tactile elements—wallpaper and fabrics—shape the design of a room."
—Judy King

Top: The great room lives up to its name. Big and cozy, the room reads well under the coffered ceiling. The black Asian coffee table lends a remarkable eclecticism to the natural tones of the room.

Bottom: A quiet, monastic-inspired corner allows the owner to focus on the task at hand. A melding of antique furnishings and fine art treasures celebrates the old and the new.

Facing Page: Our groovy teen suite was a great chance to go psychedelic. Based on the ceiling paper from London, the room explodes with orange and pink. Shag carpet, a genie lamp and a wall of album covers from the '60s and '70s create a really fun bedroom.
Photographs by Tom Grimes

"Designing spaces is truly about finding personal style."

—Judy King

A leading tastemaker who has been published and honored in noteworthy books, Robin McGarry brings a strong corporate background to her sensitive residential portfolio. She founded her firm in 1995 with decades of design experience. Today her award-winning work is sought by illustrious clientele from Connecticut to Manhattan, Washington, D.C. to Puerto Rico. The studio has masterfully transformed private offices, prestigious country clubs and exclusive residences via a buttoned-up approach: Thoughtful budgetary planning at the forefront of each project ensures a stress-free experience. Robin's hallmark style is defined by her timeless and progressive interior designs—peaceful havens of luxury and elegance—coveted by those who know.

Robin McGarry est une des plus grandes créatrices de tendances. Elle a publié des œuvres notables saluées par les critiques, et associe une solide expérience du monde des entreprises à un portfolio résidentiel caractérisé par sa sensibilité. Après plusieurs dizaines d'années d'expérience dans le domaine du design, elle a fondé sa société en 1995. Ses travaux primés sont aujourd'hui très recherchés par une clientèle illustre, du Connecticut à Manhattan, en passant par Washington et Porto Rico. Le studio a transformé de manière magistrale des bureaux privés, des country clubs prestigieux et des résidences de haut niveau à l'aide d'une approche impeccable : une planification budgétaire méthodique avant chaque projet garantit une expérience sans stress. Le style caractéristique de Robin est défini par des intérieurs à la fois intemporels et modernes, des havres de paix, de luxe et d'élégance, convoités par les connaisseurs.

Robin McGarry, una de las principales líderes de tendencia, publicada y distinguida en importantes libros, aporta sus sólidos antecedentes corporativos a su sensible cartera de clientes residenciales. Fundó su compañía en 1995, con décadas de experiencia en diseño. En la actualidad, su premiado trabajo es solicitado por una clientela ilustre desde Connecticut a Manhattan y desde Washington, D.C. a Puerto Rico. El estudio ha transformado brillantemente oficinas privadas, clubes campestres prestigiosos y residencias exclusivas a través de un enfoque formal: Una cuidadosa planificación presupuestaria en cada proyecto asegura una experiencia libre de estrés. El estilo característico de Robin está definido por sus diseños de interiores atemporales y progresivos, remansos pacíficos de lujo y elegancia, codiciados por todos los entendidos.

Robin McGarry

CONNECTICUT

Above & Left: A sparkling Venetian glass chandelier, custom silk and wool Tibetan rug and hand-polished Venetian plaster walls embrace the space with quiet opulence. Silk draperies in an Italian strung style are complemented by the chairs' gracefully tailored lines. The intimate reading nook provides a place to contemplate life: A family photograph sits on the elegant, bronze occasional table next to a black crocodile leather-bound journal that awaits reflective notes.
Photographs by Orion Bishop

Facing Page Top: In a tranquil sea of soft blue hues, the master bedroom provides a soothing respite, reminiscent of the great ocean liners of the '30s. A down-filled, silk charmeuse duvet from Bedroom Matters of Westport offers luxurious warmth for a chilly night.
Photograph by Orion Bishop

Facing Page Bottom: I designed the dining room to be a masterpiece of refined elegance. Custom Neoclassical-inspired chairs blend seamlessly with a pair of antique Tang Dynasty pottery horses from Mandarin Collection of Westport.
Photograph by Lorin Klaris Photography

Previous Page: My clients desired an ultra-glamorous, romantic master suite with elegance, classic elements and lush materials reminiscent of Old Hollywood. An original nude painting by Claudia Mengel echoes the chic, sensual ambience.
Photograph by Orion Bishop

Top & Bottom: Family members are drawn together in the delightfully unexpected dining room of their modern carriage house. The wall-mounted fireplace and custom farm table made from antique wood atop zinc bases contrasts old and new.
Photographs by Chi Chi Ubiña Photography

Facing Page: The inventive dining area magically appears when chairs on casters are pulled tableside from the 12-foot-high upholstered wall I designed with Jonathan Wagner, AIA. Located in Manhattan's legendary Gramercy Park, the elegant apartment has progressive interior architecture that makes the juxtaposition of the stunning circa 1960 Italian chandelier absolutely brilliant.
Photograph by Robert Benson Photography

"In this intensely paced technological age, it has become even more important that one's home become a place of respite. This is best achieved through the discipline of restraint, simple lines and balanced composition."

—Robin McGarry

From an early age, Kelley Proxmire knew she was destined for the world of interior design—when her friends were buying *Seventeen* magazine, she was purchasing the latest edition of *House Beautiful* and adding pieces to her cutting file. Building on more than two decades as an interior designer, Kelley has a tailored traditional style that delivers classical design with a big punch. With her firm, Kelley Interior Design, she has an established rapport among her Washington-area clientele, and her fresh take on timeless design has received numerous accolades from clients and peers alike. Crisp, bold colors paired with neutral shades provide a distinguished identity when a home has been touched by Kelley's creative vision. Her design intuition continues to lead her approach— seamlessly blending clients' cherished possessions with antique and new custom pieces acquired from her exclusive sources.

Dès son plus jeune âge, Kelley Proxmire savait qu'elle était destinée au monde de l'architecture intérieure. Alors que ses amies achetaient des magazines pour adolescentes, elle lisait déjà les derniers numéros de House Beautiful et ajoutait des pièces à sa collection d'échantillons. Après plus de vingt ans d'expérience dans le domaine de la décoration intérieure, le style de Kelley est caractérisé par une esthétique traditionnelle personnalisée à la fois classique et percutante. Avec son cabinet d'architecture intérieure, Kelley Interior Design, elle a noué de solides relations avec sa clientèle de la région de Washington, et son approche innovante de concepts intemporels est largement acclamée par ses clients comme ses collègues. L'association de couleurs vibrantes et audacieuses à des tons neutres donne une identité distinctive aux résidences touchées par la vision créative de Kelley. Son approche reste inspirée par son intuition artistique : elle incorpore de manière homogène des éléments d'ameublement antiques ou neufs en provenance de ses sources exclusives aux possessions les plus chères de ses clients.

Desde muy joven, Kelley Proxmire supo que su destino era el mundo del diseño de interiores. Mientras sus amigas compraban la revista Seventeen, ella se concentraba en la última edición de House Beautiful y a agregar imágenes a su álbum de recortes. Con más de dos décadas de experiencia como diseñadora de interiores, Kelley ha creado un estilo tradicional que brinda un diseño clásico con un enorme impacto. Con su compañía, Kelley Interior Design, ha establecido una relación de empatía con sus clientes de la región de Washington, y su novedoso enfoque de diseños clásicos ha recibido numerosos elogios tanto de sus clientes como de sus colegas. Los colores frescos y brillantes combinados con tonos neutros brindan una identidad característica a un hogar que ha recibido la visión creativa de Kelley. Su intuición de diseño continúa liderando su enfoque, combinando impecablemente las adoradas posesiones de los clientes con piezas antiguas y contemporáneas adquiridas a sus proveedores exclusivos.

Kelley Proxmire

MARYLAND

Above & Left: The Georgetown home was completely gutted and new walls and moulding were set to harmonize with the serene master bedroom. Many of the old windows were saved, which works well with the robin's egg blue walls. Silk draperies conceal a television; Roman shades give the room an enveloping feel and contribute to the bedroom acoustics. A custom acrylic and glass vanity facing east serves as a perfect place for applying makeup. The juxtaposition of old and new elements is seen with the antique gold leaf frame on the vanity. Silk shades, a ceramic lamp and a velvet chair complement the room's watercolors and art prints.
Photographs by Angie Seckinger

Facing Page Top: Everything but the red lampshades is waterproof in the open-air porch. Indoor-outdoor fabric was used and the black stripes down the sides of the draperies are Velcro for easy enclosure. To lengthen the nine-foot-wide room, white stripes were painted on a black carpet. Old wrought iron nesting tables contain board games.
Photograph by Ross Chapple

Facing Page Bottom: The summer-themed room required a new approach: a limited use of shell fabrics, straw-like sisal flooring, artificial coral above the fireplace and classic fish prints on the wall. Hidden in the valance of the bed is a television.
Photograph by Angie Seckinger

Previous Page: Set upon the Tred Avon River, the home was built in the 1860s, and my design choices respect its historical significance. River views are complemented by the cream and brown palette; the mahogany and glass lantern reproduction contribute to the traditional ambience. A faux stripe wall treatment with ribbed textures blends with the heavy linen chairs from the UK.
Photograph by Angie Seckinger

Top: The turquoise and lime green sunroom has windows on all three sides, so a bright color pattern set upon a vivid white helps give the space a pleasant disposition. Antique plates, silver shells, an orchid plant and blue and green sea glass are set upon a tabletop vignette.

Bottom: The Designers Guild chair fabric had a big and bold expression and served as the inspirational point of the room.

Facing Page: Set beside the couch is an Edward Ferrell chest. To add a burst of color alongside the white grass cloth walls, I placed a few Osage oranges next to the urn.
Photographs by Angie Seckinger

"By choosing only two or three main colors and placing them upon a neutral background, interiors can remain timeless but still exude a colorful vibrancy."
—Kelley Proxmire

Passionate about designing spaces of warmth and beauty, Lori Shinal is much more than just one of the East Coast's most artistic and exciting interior designers: She is a woman of many talents. For nearly 15 years her boutique firm, Lori Shinal Interiors, has designed an array of beautiful, engaging interiors that meld Old World charm with contemporary color and flair. Lori also designs stunning pillows featured in a nationwide collection by Barneys as well as an eclectic collection of bags, pillows and throws: *taylor by Lori Shinal*. Despite her many successful endeavors, Lori still finds time to create exquisite interiors and take buying trips to New York and Europe with clients to find the perfect piece—she believes that, most importantly, the design process should be absolute fun for the client.

Lori Shinal est passionnée par la création d'espaces empreints de chaleur et de beauté. Il ne s'agit pas seulement d'une des décoratrices les plus artistiques et les plus intéressantes de la Côte Est. C'est une femme aux multiples talents. Depuis presque 15 ans, sa société et boutique, Lori Shinal Interiors, conçoit des intérieurs séduisants et élégants, mêlant le charme du Vieux monde à la couleur et au style contemporains. Lori a également créé des coussins éblouissants repris dans une collection nationale par Barneys, ainsi qu'une collection éclectique de sacs, coussins et couvertures : Taylor par Lori Shinal. En plus de la direction de nombreuses entreprises qui connaissent un grand succès, Lori trouve encore le temps de créer des intérieurs exquis et de voyager à New York et en Europe avec des clients à la recherche de l'élément parfait. Pour elle, ce qui importe par-dessus tout, c'est que le processus de création soit source de divertissement et d'un grand plaisir pour le client.

Una apasionada del diseño de espacios calidos y bellos, Lori Shinal es mucho más que una de las diseñadoras de interiores más artísticas e interesantes de la Costa Este: se trata de una mujer de muchos talentos. Durante casi 15 años, su compañía boutique, Lori Shinal Interiors, ha diseñado una variedad de bellos y atractivos interiores que combinan los encantos de viejo mundo con el color y la elegancia contemporáneos. Lori también diseña extraordinarias almohadas, incluidas en una colección a nivel nacional de Barneys, así como también una ecléctica colección de carteras, almohadas y cobertores: Taylor by Lori Shinal. A pesar de sus muchas actividades exitosas, Lori aún tiene tiempo para crear interiores exquisitos y realizar viajes de compras a Nueva York y Europa con sus clientes, en búsqueda de la pieza perfecta. Está convencida de que, sobre todo, el proceso de diseño debe resultar muy divertido al cliente.

Lori Shinal

PENNSYLVANIA

Above: I mixed antiques with furniture of a more tailored aesthetic for a Philadelphia condominium in an Old World-style building; the drum chandelier made of shell is a favorite piece. The upholstery and lamps are from Ed Gray of Bruges Home.

Facing Page Top: We installed the herringbone floor and transformed an unfinished basement into a fabulous wine cellar; we found the centerpiece, an antique French table, on a buying trip and Amy Baxter draped the ceiling with fabric.

Facing Page Bottom Left: The dressing room features a handpainted floor, plaster ceiling and five custom paintings inspired by a love of sailing and the water, all by Meg Shattuck Studio; the exquisite millwork is by Milacci Custom Woodworking.

Facing Page Bottom Right: The antique chest is topped by my client's treasured collection of Lalique fish and amazing flowers by Danuta Knobloch and Hope Boccardo of H&D Design.

Previous Page: The Jacques Garcia table is ideal for entertaining, with ample seating via custom-made chairs and cherished loveseats for two. The room's chartreuse and chocolate brown palette contrasts splendidly with the silver Venetian plaster ceiling by John Ferris Decorative Painting; the flowers are by H&D Design.
Photographs by Jeffrey Totaro

"Homes should be reflections of their owners that are conducive to their lifestyle and the product of their travels, passions and special memories."

—Lori Shinal

Top: I found the vintage shutters in Provence and installed them inside for a wonderful interplay of bringing the outdoors in. I'm always known for a splash of red so I used the red table with antique chairs around it; Tole chandelier and Etro fabric on the windows complete the composition.

Center: We used the clients' cherished pieces to create a relaxing den in an Old World-style condominium, then stained the floors darker and painted the walls red for the perfect drama that the client was looking for.

Bottom: We used a handpainted sink and tiles in the poolhouse bathroom; John Ferris Decorative Painting did all the woodwork and the cubbies in distressed blue to match the tile.

Facing Page Top: On a New York trip we found the capitals supporting the amazing sideboard and I designed the marble top, which supports a pair of 18th-century candelabras. Guests love the drapes that appear as ball gowns; the flowers are by H&D Design.

Facing Page Bottom: We transformed the living room into a billiard room that is used almost every day. The walls, upholstered in ultrasuede, are accented with special detail taping and nailheads; the Italian light fixtures complement the room impeccably.
Photographs by Jeffrey Totaro

chapter two

chapitre deux

capítulo dos

Southeast

Above: Douglas Weiss, page 266

Innately talented and worldly, Jeffrey Adkisson has become one of Nashville's stars on the interior design scene. The principal of Adkisson Design, Jeffrey is a Vanderbilt graduate who was privileged to study at Parsons Paris School of Art & Design. A true Anglophile with a passion for touring England's gracious period homes for inspiration, he visits many European design capitals on shopping excursions, seeking fine art, antiques, lighting and accessories. Travel often influences his creative work in both new home interiors and historical renovations. Homeowners appreciate his artful eye and 30 years' experience in art direction of spaces, selecting proper building components and working with clients' needs and desires: the end result being a timeless, magical living space. His ability to capture a vision, organize and edit is his secret to success. This thoughtful interior designer takes care in creating classical and contemporary homes to express individual style while providing glorious backdrops for living.

Grâce à son talent et sa sophistication innés, Jeffrey Adkisson est devenu l'une des stars de Nashville sur la scène de la décoration intérieure. À la tête d'Adkisson Design, Jeffrey est diplômé de Vanderbilt et a eu le privilège d'étudier à la Parsons School of Art & Design de Paris. Authentique anglophile animé d'une passion pour la visite des résidences de l'ère victorienne d'Angleterre pour y trouver l'inspiration, il se rend régulièrement dans de nombreuses capitales de la création européenne pour y faire des achats, à la recherche d'œuvres d'art, d'antiquités, d'éléments d'éclairage et d'accessoires. Ces voyages influencent souvent son œuvre créative dans le cadre d'intérieurs de maisons neuves et de rénovations historiques. Les propriétaires sont séduits par son sens artistique et ses 30 années d'expérience dans le domaine de la direction artistique des espaces, son choix des matériaux de construction les plus adaptés et son écoute des besoins et des souhaits de ses clients. Le résultat en est un cadre de vie intemporel et magique. Son secret réside dans sa capacité à capturer une vision, à l'organiser et à la modifier. Ce décorateur d'intérieur intelligent prend soin de créer des résidences classiques et contemporaines qui sont l'expression d'un style individuel et constituent des cadres de vie élégants.

Con un talento y sofisticación innatos, Jeffrey Adkisson se ha convertido en una de las estrellas de Nashville en el mundo del diseño de interiores. Jeffrey, el director de Adkisson Design, es un graduado de Vanderbilt quien tuvo el privilegio de estudiar en la Escuela de Arte y Diseño Parsons de Paris. Un verdadero anglófilo con una pasión por las visitas de hogares de época de Inglaterra en búsqueda de inspiración, recorre diversas capitales de diseño europeas en excursiones de compras, en búsqueda de piezas de arte, antigüedades, luces y accesorios. A menudo sus viajes ejercen una influencia en su trabajo creativo, tanto en los interiores de hogares nuevos como en remodelaciones históricas. Los propietarios valoran su ojo artístico y sus 30 años de experiencia en la dirección artística de espacios, seleccionando los componentes de construcción adecuados y trabajando con las necesidades y deseos de los clientes: el resultado final es un espacio habitable atemporal y mágico. Su habilidad para capturar una visión, organizar y editar constituye el secreto de su éxito. Este considerado diseñador de interiores pone especial atención en la creación de hogares clásicos y contemporáneos que expresar un estilo individual al mismo tiempo que brindar una gloriosa escenografía para vivir.

Jeffrey Adkisson

Above Left: Welcoming guests with antiquities and a sense of edited grandeur, an oval foyer embraces all who enter with handpainted yellow damask walls underscored by inlaid stone flooring. The antique French tapestry, Dutch burled elm table and Queen Anne chair are illuminated by a pair of newly crafted gilded sconces.

Above Right: We renovated a ranch home to great heights with its impressive 22-foot ceilings, graced by one bespoke 10-foot crystal chandelier. The regal Queen Anne table with authentic, original tapestry chairs allows for sumptuous dining day and night. Hand-waxed Venetian plaster walls are formally accented by luxurious red and gold striped silk draperies.

Facing Page: Bathing by fire glow is pure indulgence. The quaint limestone fireplace anchors a dramatic 14-foot stone wall in the master bath, creating a subtle spa atmosphere. The original chimney structure and wall were incorporated in the new addition. Marble vanities, a Roman tub and gleaming fixtures create sparkle and illusion.

Previous Page: A 90-year-old English country living room is an elegant mélange of fine antique furnishings enveloped in soothing, muted tones. The carved poplar fireplace, Malayer Persian rug and silk portiere draperies relate well to the 19th-century pastoral painting and English tapestry armchair. Fresh bouquets fill the room with fragrance while bringing the vibrant garden indoors.

Photographs by Sanford Myers

"I love to create beautiful, comfortable and dignified backdrops for real life."
—Jeffrey Adkisson

Above: The French tapestry was inspiration for the elegant sitting room. Shelter sofas embrace guests in luxury beside the limestone fireplace. Period antique pieces were acquired from jaunts to England. Imare Oriental porcelain vases flank both sides of the mantel. Soft handpainted striae walls of pale aqua and gold crest upward to a barrel-vaulted ceiling.

Facing Page Top: A spacious gourmet kitchen becomes intimate with its broken cherry wood island featuring polished granite countertops. Authentic barley twist stools from England and a French farm table with Windsor chairs sits atop the herringbone-patterned Jerusalem limestone floor. An antique French chandelier hovers above for charming country ambience.

Facing Page Bottom: A formal invitation to gracious dining is simply irresistible amidst handpainted silk wall coverings imported from England. We created a quintessential floral backdrop for the magnificent custom Russian-inspired crystal chandelier highlighting the residents' heirloom Queen Anne table and chairs.
Photographs by Sanford Myers

"Art is very important . . . become knowledgeable and enjoy searching for great finds."

—Jeffrey Adkisson

Top: A prized 18th-century carved walnut sideboard is flanked by William and Mary knife boxes, rare English pewter plates. Sheffield candlestick lamps are centered by an 1800s' Dutch painting and Chinese Sung Dynasty earthenware goldfish, resulting in a tranquil mood.

Center: Art makes an immediate statement in the two-story, sun-drenched foyer. We discovered the circa 1850s' oil painting in an attic. The 1600s' French Britton table of a hand-carved flautist brings a touch of whimsy. The new wrought iron and bronze handrail design was inspired from Spanish ironwork.

Bottom: An unexpected 15-foot-long hallway becomes home to a period 18th-century English mule chest and wet bar with barley twist motif cabinetry. Ubba tuba granite counters reflect organic tones, and the English wall screen's cordovan colors are mirrored in the imported faux crocodile tile backsplash.

Facing Page: We made the rich mahogany fireplace a focal point framed by Italian red damask upholstered walls. A rare Russian painting echoes the woodlands outside of the home and evokes a sense of mystery. Old World craftsmanship and honest materials create comfort and a relaxed, yet dignified aesthetic.

Photographs by Sanford Myers

Whether designing interiors for a waterfront primary residence, a desert retreat or an apartment in Paris, Linda Burnside of LGB Interiors starts with the pieces her clients love best. She has a knack for elevating somewhat ordinary objects to fine art status, allowing them to inspire the design. Sculptures or paintings from her clients' travels are admittedly Linda's preferred starting places, but she can express her creativity from practically anything. Linda is drawn to natural materials and motifs and incorporates them in almost every project, quipping that she is "an organic designer." An eco-friendly undertaking in North Carolina furthers the point, but in a different direction: She designed the home's interiors using a limited palette of recycled materials. Whatever the parameters of the project, Linda takes her signature passionate approach, believing that people should not settle for liking their home—they should absolutely love it.

Qu'il s'agisse d'une résidence principale en bord de mer, d'une retraite dans le désert ou d'un appartement à Paris, Linda Burnside de LGB Interiors travaille autour des pièces préférées de ses clients. Elle sait faire d'objets plutôt ordinaires de véritables œuvres d'arts susceptibles d'inspirer ses créations. Les sculptures ou les peintures glanées par ses clients au cours de leurs voyages sont les points d'ancrage que Linda aime choisir pour ses créations, mais elle peut exprimer sa créativité à partir de n'importe quel élément. Linda est séduite par les matières et les motifs de la nature. Elle les incorpore à presque tous ses projets et se qualifie en plaisantant de « créatrice organique ». Un projet respectueux de la nature en Caroline du Nord en témoigne encore, dans une direction différente toutefois : elle en a conçu la décoration intérieure à l'aide d'une palette de matériaux recyclés. Quels que soient les paramètres du projet, Linda l'aborde avec l'approche passionnée qui la caractérise, forte de sa conviction selon laquelle il ne faut pas se contenter d'aimer sa maison, il faut absolument l'adorer.

Ya sea diseñando interiores para una residencia principal en la costa, un refugio en el desierto o un departamento en París, Linda Burnside de LGB Interiors comienza con las piezas preferidas de sus clientes. Tiene la capacidad de convertir objetos relativamente comunes en piezas de arte, haciendo posible que inspiren el diseño. Las esculturas o pinturas provenientes de los viajes de sus clientes constituyen su punto de partida preferido, aunque es capaz de expresar su creatividad a partir de cualquier otro objeto. Linda siente atracción por los materiales y motivos naturales y los incorpora en casi todos sus proyectos, sosteniendo jocosamente que ella es una "diseñadora orgánica". Como prueba, aunque en un sentido diferente, existe un proyecto respetuoso del medioambiente en Carolina del Norte: Diseñó los interiores del hogar utilizando un catálogo limitado de materiales reciclados. Independientemente de los parámetros del proyecto, Linda utiliza su apasionado enfoque característico, su convencimiento de que las personas no deben conformarse con que su hogar les resulte agradable, debe resultarles absolutamente adorable.

Linda Burnside

SOUTH CAROLINA

Above Left & Right: I've done quite a bit of resort and vacation home design but when the owners of the Palmetto Bluff home showed me their property and its views, I'd never seen anything quite as beautiful—the locale provided plenty of design inspiration. The master bedroom's seating nook overlooks the May River; it's a great place to people watch and enjoy the yachts coming in and going out. The master bath is pure luxury, with a profusion of marble, cabinetry finished in a soft French blue, pebble flooring in the shower and custom vanities that read like built-in armoires.

Facing Page Top: When rooms are infused with natural light, I like to go with vivid wall colors. For the sunroom, I chose a rich chocolate brown with yellow and cream accents; the adjacent living room has complementary yellow walls with brown accents. The whole design is a study in contrast with most elements exuding natural qualities: fabrics with organic motifs, a woven sumac rug, lamps with coral-like bases and leaf art prints.

Facing Page Bottom: The dining room doors open to a balcony, so I chose a round table to create a nice flow for entertaining—guests can mingle inside or out without straying too far from the heart of the party. The homeowners wanted the house to be elegant but comfortable, and I achieved that aesthetic by marrying traditional décor with the steel blue, faux finished walls and chairs upholstered in a wonderful velvet stripe.

Previous Page: The homeowner had a unique request—especially considering he is a bachelor. He wanted a living room that didn't revolve around the television. I featured his hunting interest, his Costa Rican heritage—the art—and created a welcoming yet masculine space with oversized leather chairs and a nature-inspired color scheme.
Photographs by Robert Clark

"Every single room should have at least one original work of art."

—Linda Burnside

"Only acquire pieces you love. And if you own something you don't love, it's okay to let it go."

—Linda Burnside

Above: The Palmetto Bluff residence is called The Boathouse, and the homeowners wanted to nod to that idea without turning it into a gaudy theme. Thoughtful accents like the canoe bookshelf, upholstery by Osborne & Little and sandy-colored wall treatment culminate for a sophisticated coastal look. There's also a bit of Low Country charm woven into the space.

Facing Page: It seems unlikely, but the interior design of The Boathouse began with the fabulous granite countertop. I found the piece in Atlanta and it immediately reminded me of the view you get flying over the Bahamas—varying shades of water interspersed by islands of warm sand. I built the whole kitchen around the granite and it just sort of spread from there—into the adjacent living room and then everywhere else. The bar stools echo its natural quality and so does the cabinetry. I chose the drop lights for their lantern-like feel and diffused glow; the four lights in the cove ceiling are shaped like portholes, continuing the nautical motif.
Photographs by Robert Clark

Right: The guestroom was fairly small, so I visually expanded the space by adding a punch of color with an accent wall. All of the décor has a nice organic theme: the artwork, throw pillows, rug, accent pieces, even the fan. My travels to Singapore snuck into the design a little bit, too.

Facing Page Top: When I design backsplashes, I never use just one tile—I like to mix textures and colors for depth and richness. The backsplash of tumbled marble and onyx, gold-colored marble countertop and distressed cabinetry perfectly complement one another. I incorporated the homeowners' cherished collection of mismatched chairs around the dining table; it's a twist of the unexpected and adds authenticity. I kept the composition of the adjacent living room really clean so it feels like a picture, framed by the arched doorway. The art above the fireplace inspired the color palette of cheery yellows and corals.

Facing Page Bottom: The room's design carefully balances light and dark, old and new. Silver accents nicely punctuate the prevailing gold tones.
Photographs by Robert Clark

"Rooms that look like they should be roped off in a museum just aren't my style. Interiors should strike a perfect balance between exciting and practical."
—Linda Burnside

You would have to be insanely passionate about your profession to pull off the kind of work habits that Monique delaHoussaye-Breaux enthusiastically manages to orchestrate. The coordination is enormous, for Posh Exclusive Interiors is almost a concierge service. Never in one place very long, Monique and her team successfully utilize tight plans to allow for one complete install; her firm once moved a 25,000-square-foot home in two days—from expected interior elements like furniture and artwork to clothes on hangers, folded towels, stocked pantries and chef-approved accoutrements. Once Monique's creative mind has the canvas painted, the countless design variables that she manages quickly evolve into a sophisticated setting in which the homeowner could have a dinner party the very evening Monique's trucks depart. There is a calculated method to this madness. Turns out that Monique is insanely passionate with what she does, and it shows.

Il faudrait vraiment être passionné par sa profession à un point proche de la folie pour adopter des habitudes de travail telles que celles que Monique delaHoussaye-Breaux parvient à orchestrer avec enthousiasme. Le travail de coordination est énorme, dans la mesure où Posh Exclusive Interiors est presque un service de conciergerie. Monique et son équipe, qui ne restent jamais au même endroit très longtemps, mettent en œuvre avec succès des plans très ambitieux permettant une installation complète. Sa société a déjà déménagé une maison de 2322 mètres carrés en deux jours, des éléments d'intérieur habituels tels que des meubles et des œuvres d'arts, aux vêtements sur les cintres, aux serviettes bien pliées, aux gardes mangers remplis de provisions, en passant par les accessoires approuvés par le chef. Lorsque l'esprit créatif de Monique a conçu le cadre de vie, les innombrables variables de création qu'elle gère évoluent rapidement en un environnement sophistiqué dans lequel le propriétaire de la maison peut organiser un dîner le soir même du départ du camion de Monique. Sa folie est calculée. C'est que Monique est follement passionnée par ce qu'elle fait, et cela se voit.

Para lograr los hábitos de trabajo que Monique delaHoussaye-Breaux es capaz de poner en práctica entusiastamente hace falta sentir una pasión desenfrenada por la profesión. La coordinación es fenomenal, ya que Posh Exclusive Interiors es casi un servicio de asistencia personal. Monique y su equipo nunca permanecen mucho tiempo en el mismo lugar y utilizan con éxito una planificación cuidadosa para dar cuenta de una instalación completa; en una ocasión, su compañía mudó un hogar de 25.000 pies cuadrados en dos días, incluyendo elementos interiores clásicos como muebles y obras de arte, y otros que no lo son tanto como ropa, colgadores, toallas dobladas, despensas completas y equipamiento de cocina. Una vez que su mente creativa ha completado el lienzo, las innumerables variables de diseño que maneja rápidamente se convierten en un entorno sofisticado en el que el propietario puede organizar una cena suntuosa la misma tarde en que parten los camiones de la mudanza. Existe un método calculado en tal locura. Monique siente una enorme pasión por todo lo que hace, y se nota.

Monique delaHoussaye-Breaux

LOUISIANA

Above: The 50-year-old Italian estate's rooms were enormous, and we needed suitable furniture to accentuate the scale. The owner called me about the home he and his wife just bought, stating, "I think it has good bones." He was right on target. We custom-designed everything to scale, from the furniture to the filigree moulding, truly turning an ugly duckling into a swan. We called the guest bedroom the Marilyn Monroe Room—we always imagined her walking out of it.

Left: Custom-designed cabinets and Italian glass wall tile was selected to complement the fabric that is repeated in the guest bedroom window.

Facing Page Top: Bronzes, coppers, tans and taupes—the Italian exterior required a logical color palette; good design flows from the exterior in.

Facing Page Bottom: Everything works together. Color meets texture on the walls, which adds essential richness. A custom-made rug fills the space, framing the scale, pulling the whole thing together by making it cozier.

Previous Page: We started the project fresh, with nothing holding us back. All projects are special in their own right, but renovations—when the owner can see a transformation take place—are truly fulfilling. This ideal homeowner had a great level of trust, and carte blanche is always hard to beat.
Photographs by Chipper Hatter

"I don't expect happy accidents—we work too hard to rely on whimsy."
—Monique delaHoussaye-Breaux

Above: I was on a plane with a client, who handed me a set of plans for a private hangar, asking me to handle the design of the project. There is a certain level of comfort to be had before boarding the plane, and I wanted make sure that comfort was met.

Facing Page Top & Bottom: The rich, dark-wood cabinetry coupled with a marble and glass bar are an occurrence of traditional meeting contemporary. The hangar was coated in pearl white to give the plane a pristine appearance. This was another one of those projects of creative freedom—the owner never saw anything beforehand.
Photographs by Chipper Hatter

"Psychology plays a huge hand in interior design. A good designer should be able to read a homeowner very quickly."
—Monique delaHoussaye-Breaux

Top: I knew going in that we had to accommodate a large family, with several individuals over a range of ages. With breakfast being the most important meal of the day, I made sure that adequate bar space allowed for family meals.

Bottom: The powder room is a fine example of the middle ground for which the design called. Despite the sleekness of the pedestal sink, the dark woods and the rugs throughout, the home is complementary of the transitional style we were trying to achieve.

Facing Page: A lot of clients consult us before they purchase residences. With a Florida penthouse, we selected the perfect home with the best views. Though there are great intimate spaces, we made sure there was plenty of room to support a big family—with a sofa that can seat a dozen people. This high attention to detail is the ground upon which Posh was founded.
Photographs by Chipper Hatter

For Barry Dixon, interior design is a simple balancing act. He mixes the old with the new, the East with the West, the interior with the exterior, and on and on. When designing, he knows that pieces of the past should come forward reverently to a vibrant present. His cross-cultural perspective began as a child, living in India, Korea, New Caledonia and South Africa. This afforded him a global perspective and laid the foundation for his future; more than half of Barry's work these days is implemented abroad. Developing his distinct world flavor, Barry has established his own line of furniture, fabrics and rugs—giving him the ability to offer his signature flair through multiple mediums. What do all of his spaces have in common? Balance, history and simple, organic beauty.

Pour Barry Dixon, la décoration intérieure est un exercice d'équilibre qui consiste à associer l'ancien et le nouveau, l'Est et l'Ouest, l'intérieur et l'extérieur, et ainsi de suite. Lorsqu'il crée, il sait que les éléments du passé doivent s'intégrer de manière respectueuse à un présent vibrant. Il a acquis la perspective interculturelle qui a servi de fondation à son avenir alors qu'il était enfant, en Inde, en Corée, en Nouvelle-Calédonie et en Afrique du Sud. Plus de la moitié des œuvres de Barry ont été créées à l'étranger. Barry a lancé sa propre ligne de meubles, de textiles et de tapis à l'influence internationale distincte, de sorte qu'il peut proposer sa griffe sous de multiples formes. Qu'est-ce que tous ces espaces ont en commun ? Équilibre, histoire, et la simple beauté organique.

Para Barry Dixon, el diseño de interiores es un simple acto de malabarismo. Combina lo nuevo con lo viejo, Oriente con Occidente, lo interior con lo exterior y así indefinidamente. Cuando diseña, es conciente de que las piezas del pasado deben avanzar reverentemente hacia un presente vibrante. Su perspectiva intercultural se remonta a su niñez, durante los años que pasó en la India, Corea, Nueva Caledonia y Sudáfrica. Esos años le permitieron adquirir una perspectiva global y sentar las bases de su futuro; más de la mitad de sus obras son implementadas en el extranjero. Desarrollando su particular cualidad internacional, Barry ha creado su propia línea de muebles, telas y alfombras que le proporciona la capacidad de ofrecer su estilo característico a través de múltiples elementos. ¿Cuáles son los elementos en común de todos sus espacios? Equilibrio, historia y una belleza simple y orgánica.

Barry Dixon

VIRGINIA

"My interest lies in the evolution of design and form. It's important to keep an eye toward what may become classic, completely aware of the fact that design is a constantly changing continuum."

—Barry Dixon

Above: Perched on a cliffside, the home ushers the outside in. Over-scaled lamps and a Dana oval ottoman juxtaposed with an under-scaled Drake sofa—from my self-titled collection for Tomlinson/Erwin-Lambeth—make for an unexpected sense of simplicity. Playing the 1930s' vibe of the gilded lounge chairs against the natural teak-carved taborets works beautifully when properly paired.
Photograph by Tria Giovan, courtesy of Southern Accents *magazine*

Right: Details can take center stage: Bergamo embroidery atop Rubelli silk panels catches the eye, drawing attention to the high level of skilled craftsmanship.
Photograph by Tria Giovan, courtesy of Southern Accents *magazine*

Facing Page: The outdoors become elegant; John Robshaw translucent silk bed hangings and Robert Kime hand-printed silk panels bring an organic quality to the room in the Virginia mountain home.
Photograph by Tria Giovan, courtesy of Southern Accents *magazine*

Previous Page: Hand-colored, 18th-century leather-bound book plate engravings act as shutters at the end of a library, repeating the grid-work of the custom iron railing. The rustic French chandelier looming above measures five feet tall.
Photograph by Tria Giovan, courtesy of Veranda *magazine*

Above: In a 19th-century Georgetown study, a bold masculine temperament prevails. Worldly and contemporary features are streamlined with thoughtful geometric balance. A lacquered Chinese table and a vibrant Gene Davis painting help create the modern yet relaxed room.
Photograph by Gordon Beall

Facing Page Top: With its hazy dream-like murals, a Maryland home boasts 17th-century Venetian Doges chairs and an 18th-century Dutch leather screen. The seagrass carpet becomes a crucial element, undercutting formality and fussiness. The femininity of the room is balanced by a strong Moroccan pendant lamp in the background, found in a Marrakesh market, and low bronze tables from Baker.
Photograph by Tria Giovan, courtesy of Veranda *magazine*

Facing Page Bottom: Boomerang chairs, a custom-made Tibetan carpet and brilliant hues make up a warm room with austere elements. Iron rods circumnavigating the room bear simple linen drapery panels, accenting the space's one-of-a-kind pieces. The painting, for instance, is an inherited work belonging to the homeowner.
Photograph by Tria Giovan, courtesy of Veranda *magazine*

Top: A closer look reveals rich handpainted fabrics next to a marble Vaughn lamp atop a hammered copper Odegard table.
Photograph by Tria Giovan, courtesy of Southern Accents *magazine*

Bottom: The dining room showcases a Turkish ceiling medallion behind a tabletop of Bohemian crystal and antique creamware. My version of a Queen Anne chair surrounds the table. Though reinterpreted for the 21st century, the piece retains its fundamental structure, casting the same shadow it has for generations.
Photograph by Tria Giovan, courtesy of Veranda *magazine*

Facing Page: A garden-retreat bathroom highlights the luxury of nature. An abstracted mural evokes a lush, woodsy environment while the silver-encrusted Odegard chair and pewter Waterworks soaking tub bring new definition to mineral bath. Notice the tonalities—golds against greys, stones against metals, et cetera.
Photograph by Tria Giovan, courtesy of Southern Accents *magazine*

"Rooms that begin with traditional architecture and blend styles that cross borders of time and culture yield worldly yet hospitable modern spaces."

—Barry Dixon

It must look as if it's always been there. William R. Eubanks applies this premise to all of his work, contemporary or traditional. He loves creating variety in textures, pulling together subtle patterns, choosing elegant color palettes and employing all of the customary tools of the interior design trade. Every space should be perfectly balanced, detailed and appointed, but William maintains that a space is simply incomplete without unique furnishings and art, which reveal people's personalities and interests. William is known for his savvy in weaving together beautiful interior tapestries of textiles, furnishings and art. Each piece may come from or nod to a different century or even continent, but all complement the setting and contribute to the designer's signature seasoned ambience.

On doit penser qu'il en a toujours été ainsi. William R. Eubanks applique ce principe à toutes ses œuvres, contemporaines ou traditionnelles. Il adore travailler avec des textures variées, rapprocher des compositions subtiles, choisir des palettes de couleurs élégantes, et employer tous les outils habituels de la décoration intérieure professionnelle. Chaque espace doit être parfaitement équilibré, détaillé et constitué. William assure qu'un espace est tout simplement incomplet sans meubles et œuvres d'art uniques, qui révèlent les personnalités et centres d'intérêt des gens. William est réputé pour sa capacité à tisser de merveilleuses tapisseries intérieures composées de textiles, de meubles et d'œuvres d'art. Chaque pièce peut évoquer et provenir d'un siècle ou même d'un continent différent, mais toutes sans exception complètent l'ensemble et contribuent à la création de l'ambiance sophistiquée qui fait la griffe du créateur.

Debe parecer que siempre estuvo ahí. William R. Eubanks aplica esa premisa a todo su trabajo, ya sea contemporáneo o tradicional. Adora crear variedad en texturas, construyendo patrones sutiles, seleccionando paletas de colores elegantes y utilizando todas las herramientas tradicionales del oficio de diseño de interiores. Cada espacio debe estar perfectamente equilibrado, detallado y seleccionado, pero William sostiene que un espacio no está completo si no incluye mobiliario y objetos de arte exclusivos, que revelan las personalidades y los intereses de las personas. William es conocido por su capacidad para crear bellos tapices interiores de textiles, mobiliario y objetos de arte. Cada pieza debe pertenecer o hacer referencia a un siglo o continente diferente, pero todos deben complementar el lugar y contribuir al experimentado ambiente característico del diseñador.

William R. Eubanks

FLORIDA ■ NEW YORK ■ TENNESSEE

Above: When my clients purchased their waterfront home, it was a 1970s' space in need of a facelift—thankfully it had great bones. Because the lady of the house, who soon became the ambassador to Barbados, wanted the Palm Beach residence as a winter retreat, the goal of the project was clear: create an elegant place for relaxing alone or entertaining a large crowd that showcases the homeowners' tastes. I achieved this by designing multiple seating arrangements in the living room and drew inspiration from the couple's passion for culture and travel. The vividly hued coromandel screen commands attention amidst the soft color palette.

Facing Page Top & Bottom: Frenchmen Constantin Kluge, Roger Muhl and Jules René Hervé are just a few of the artists represented. And while the art is exquisite, the true focal point is the ocean—it's like a painting, framed by the silk drapery. I utilized the homeowners' blue coral, which exudes a flame-like character in the limestone fireplace.

Previous Page: To make the long gallery more approachable, I divided it into three sections with millwork, creating an 18th-century continental space. The black granite flooring is original, but I detailed it with marble cabochons. The mahogany and parcel-gilt Regency-style console is flanked by a pair of black japanned carved side chairs.

Photographs by Kim Sargent

Top & Bottom: My clients selected the floral chintz, which set the tone. I designed the bed hangings to be light yet enveloping. The homeowners love to read, so I gave them proper nighttime illumination through a double set of lamps on each side of the bed. Because scale and comfort are very important to me, I chose a pair of Louis XV chaises at the base of the bed instead of specifying a traditional bench; the chairs are beautiful by themselves, and their tailored scale makes them functional as well. To complement the floor-to-ceiling draperies, and bring out the warmth of the antique pine desk, I selected a subdued Regency stripe wallcovering. The exquisite Nowak painting of a town square echoes the city views enjoyed from the master bedroom's terrace.

Facing Page: I am partial to circular tables, especially in square rooms, because they inspire group conversation. The warm brown and slate blue wallcovering is de Gournay handpainted, ochre-dyed silk panels, colored expressly for the space. The rare Chinese seated figures, representing various states of mind, dot the room—on the main wall, credenza and dining table. They are delightful conversation pieces and so perfect with the room's décor. I chose the silver pagoda from the homeowners' collection as a centerpiece because of its appropriate scale; it can be updated with flowers in season and of course continues the Asian theme. The beautifully carved mirror is a 20th-century piece crafted in 18th-century Venetian style; it brilliantly catches the shimmer of the bronze and rock crystal chandelier.

Previous Pages: The process of selecting fabrics is limitless; changing just one element sometimes leads to a completely different look. The library feels very warm because of the rich combination of fabrics— chintz, silk and velvet. Even though the textures are luxurious, the way they are combined ensures that the room doesn't take itself too seriously. The pattern of the club chairs echoes the four superb 19th-century Jacob George Strutt engravings that flank the large seascape by Dutch artist Bernard de Hoog. Though the room appears to be paneled in weathered wood, the effect is actually achieved through a paint and glaze combination I developed for the room. The unique backdrop combined with the color palette and the subject matter depicted in the art pays homage to the seaside theme that is ever so subtly incorporated throughout the home. A pair of turquoise 18th-century Chinese kylins with 19th-century bronze doré mounts, the exotic Indian bench inlaid with mother-of-pearl, and the delightful Ming-period terracotta figures add touches of whimsy to the space. *Photographs by Kim Sargent*

"I always love a bit of rock crystal. It's good feng shui."
—William R. Eubanks

Cecil Hayes' dynamic approach to interior design began more than three decades ago, and her love and commitment to the craft has only become more fervent. She asserts that interior design, with its countless possibilities and evolution, continues to get more exciting every day. Since her debut in the 1970s, Cecil has earned prominence among the South Florida interior design community with spectacular projects that span the United States and the globe. Her style and uncanny ability to envision the amazing possibilities in any genre and in any space, ground-up work or existing, have earned Cecil a rightful place among the most sought-after interior designers today. The principal of Cecil's Designers Unlimited has also distinguished herself as the first African American interior designer to be recognized worldwide. In 2002, she founded The Mikala Collection, her signature luxury furniture line consisting of case goods and upholstery.

L'approche dynamique de l'architecture intérieure de Cecil Hayes a vu le jour il y a plus de trente ans, mais son amour et son dévouement à cet art sont sans cesse plus fervents. Pour elle, l'architecture intérieure, en évolution constante et caractérisée par d'innombrables possibilités, est chaque jour plus passionnante. Depuis ses débuts dans les années 1970, Cecil s'est distinguée au sein de la communauté des décorateurs d'intérieur du sud de la Floride grâce à des projets spectaculaires dans l'ensemble des États-Unis et le monde entier. Son style et sa capacité troublante à envisager des possibilités surprenantes, quel que soit le genre ou l'espace, qu'il s'agisse de création pure ou de travail sur des éléments existants, ont valu à Cecil une place bien méritée parmi les décorateurs les plus en vue actuellement. La directrice de Designers Unlimited, l'entreprise de Cecil, s'est également distinguée comme la première décoratrice d'intérieur afro-américaine reconnue dans le monde entier. En 2002, elle a fondé la Collection Mikala, sa ligne d'ameublement de luxe composée de meubles de rangement et tapissés.

El dinámico enfoque al diseño de interiores de Cecil Hayes comenzó hace más de tres décadas, y su amor y dedicación al arte se ha convertido en más ferviente. Considera que el diseño de interiores, con sus infinitas posibilidades y evolución, es cada día más interesante. Desde sus comienzos en la década del 70, Cecil se ha destacado en la comunidad de diseño de interiores del sur de Florida, con proyectos espectaculares en EEUU y el resto del mundo. Su estilo y su extraordinaria habilidad para adelantarse a las asombrosas posibilidades en cualquier género y espacio, con una obra nueva o una existente, le ha otorgado un merecido lugar entre los más codiciados diseñadores de interiores de la actualidad. La directora de Cecil's Designers Unlimited también se ha distinguido por convertirse en la primera diseñadora de interiores afroamericana de reconocimiento internacional. En 2002 fundó la Colección Mikala, su característica línea de muebles de lujo que incluye mobiliario de almacenaje y tapicería.

Cecil Hayes

FLORIDA

Above: The minute I saw a beautiful Indonesian screen during one of my trips, I knew it would make a great headboard for the right interior. Bedrooms have the ability to incorporate many different textiles and should. We placed a Tuscan quilt on the master bed and ornamented it with a Kuba cloth, which is made from very fine raffia by the Kuba people of the Congo. We always consider interesting ways to use beautiful and comment-worthy antique pieces: The bench is actually an antique African bed.

Facing Page: A smooth limestone fireplace is a remarkable crowning piece in a room, especially juxtaposed against a carved mantel. The challenge was to balance the ethnic pieces of art properly within the context of the room. Working with pieces the couple already loved, I added an exotic ceiling chandelier, which causes the eye to travel up to the groin ceiling and then down again to fully appreciate and absorb the elements of the room.

Previous Page: I was involved in the conception and construction of a Boca Raton vacation home for an avid art collecting couple. The lighting of carefully placed niches was integral to the overall interior design of their home; we wanted to perfectly highlight the amazing pieces of art without our placements appearing too overt. Integrating a mixed media of dark and neutral woods and metals paired with posh area rugs softened the feel of the room, while incorporating a neutral palette allowed the paintings to be the focus. We did not want to diminish the overall effect of the space, therefore very few additional items were added to the Portuguese dining room table of complementary wood and iron.
Photographs by Kim Sargent

"It is important to first discover the spirit of the home in order to best design for it."
—Cecil Hayes

"Spaces should be beautiful but they should also fit their owner's lifestyle. No room is meant to be simply enjoyed from afar—it must be lived in."

—Cecil Hayes

Above: Another exciting and rewarding part of my vocation is that I get the opportunity to work with many different people, mediums and those corresponding styles that are wrought as a result. For a young bachelor with very sophisticated taste, a more hip and masculine design was in order. We decided on contemporary furnishings and art with serviceable built-ins to accommodate his lifestyle and interests. The column-bracing built-in, crafted of ash wood and glass shelving, displays artful glass pieces and also has a secret door housing the owner's extensive DVD collection.

Facing Page Top: No bachelor's home would be complete without a state-of-the-art game room. Designed for a well-known NFL player who wanted to proudly display his team jerseys, the game room makes an obvious counterpart to the home theater room.

Facing Page Bottom: Home theaters have certain requirements in common like superior audio and acoustical materials. However, it was my challenge to also make a room that could stand on its own. The color palette was a bit bolder and more fun in fitting with the context. I chose to break up the acoustic wall panels with metal columns ornamented by sconces.
Photographs by Kim Sargent

"For great design to happen, the mind must be open to the possibilities. That is what I do for my clients. I get to know them well and guide them through the possibilities."

—Cecil Hayes

Top: There are numerous ways to affect an interesting and unique division of rooms, which invites the ability to create grand entrances. Using interestingly shaped Japanese ash wood columns, we created a grand entrance from the living to the dining room alongside a stainless steel water feature. I love mixing textures and materials for significance. Texture is one of those elements that can exist in textiles, art and even in a wall effect. I sandblasted a span of glass and contrasted it with two large, smooth sconces. With all of these soothing and permanent fixtures in the living room, the space required comfortable yet elegant furnishings. Supple leather chairs and couches in dimensions that are in balance with the room create an environment that begs to be enjoyed, not just appreciated.

Bottom: It is always nice to have one conversation starter in a room whether that may be a painting, sculpture or something even more unusual. My client never tires of talking about his coffee table, which was crafted from the engine of a plane. Similarly, the serpentine sofa is unique in that the divisions actually function to make the 18-foot couch flexible in order to shape it into a semicircle or straight line.

Facing Page Top: A master bedroom should truly be a soothing and serene place. I like the effect of light neutral tones punctuated by bursts of color in art or small accent pieces. We chose some really amazing Italian furniture to complete the look as well. The imported bed not only has clean, attractive lines accented by supple leather, the headboard actually adjusts for comfort. The bedside tables are from my own collection, topped with chiseled glass and backlit for added dimension. The bed is elevated and lit from underneath, bringing the eye around the entire room. The leather furnishings are made to be used and enjoyed; each includes a hidden mechanism that will transform the chair to a lounger.

Facing Page Bottom: To complete his idea of a poolside oasis, the homeowner wanted to have a tiki hut built. Adjacent to a pool cave, the tiki hut is surrounded by a koi pond. Only Seminole Indians are permitted to construct authentic tiki huts made of overlapping palmetto leaves and natural logs. The engineering and workmanship is amazing: In five years this hut has never leaked, and it even withstood a hurricane. Keeping in mind that we needed weather-resistant materials that would also be attractive, we chose water- and mildew-proof Sunbrella fabrics for the couches. Teakwood is a wonderful choice for outdoor wood furnishings. We chose a teakwood dinette set that we knew would age well in any weather condition.
Photographs by Kim Sargent

J. Banks Design Group thrives on the diversity of its projects: pieds-à-terre, seaside estates, resort hotels, restored farmhouses and ski lodges, among others. The firm even has experience designing castle interiors in Tuscany. Led by Joni Vanderslice, the team of J. Banks designers has earned a reputation for inventing timeless designs with a little bit of attitude—luxury without pretense. They always seem to find a pleasing balance between comfortable and sophisticated, drawing on their furniture, fabric, rug and accessory design expertise to achieve their signature tailored look; pieces are always perfectly scaled and styled to the room. With a dozen creative minds hard at work—and having fun—on projects across North America and overseas, the studio is never short on fresh ideas. Joni and her team have a continuous flow of original, inspired creations.

Le groupe J. Banks Design Group est dynamisé par le diversité de ses projets : des pieds à terre, domaines de bord de mer, des centres de villégiature, des fermes restaurées et des chalets de ski, entre autres. La société justifie même d'expérience dans le domaine de la création d'intérieurs en Toscane. Sous la direction de Joni Vanderslice, l'équipe de décorateurs de J. Banks est réputée pour ses créations intemporelles agrémentées de caractère, luxueuses sans être prétentieuses. Elles semblent toujours trouver un équilibre plaisant entre le confort et la sophistication, grâce à l'expertise en matière de conception d'ameublement, de textiles, de tapis et d'accessoires qui caractérise leur style personnalisé : L'échelle et le style des éléments d'ameublement sont toujours parfaitement adaptés à la pièce. Une douzaine d'esprits créatifs travaillent dans une ambiance décontractée sur des projets dans l'ensemble de l'Amérique du Nord et à l'étranger, et le studio n'est jamais à court d'idées inventives. Joni et son équipe ne cessent de produire des créations originales et inspirées.

La prosperidad de J. Banks Design Group está directamente relacionada a la diversidad de sus proyectos: viviendas secundarias, propiedades costeras, complejos hoteleros, granjas restauradas y cabañas de esquí, entre otros. La experiencia de la compañía incluye el diseño de interiores de castillos en la Toscana. Liderado por Joni Vanderslice, el equipo de diseñadores de J. Banks se ha hecho de una reputación de creación de diseños atemporales con algo de actitud: lujo sin simulación. Suelen siempre encontrar un equilibrio adecuado entre lo confortable y lo sofisticado, echando mano a su experiencia de diseño de muebles, telas, alfombras y accesorios para lograr su aspecto personalizado característico; el estilo y la escala de los elementos es siempre perfectamente acorde al ambiente. Con un equipo de doce mentes creativas dedicadas al trabajo, y disfrutando cada momento, en proyectos en toda America del Norte, el estudio nunca sufre de un faltante de ideas nuevas. Joni y su equipo generan un flujo continuo de creaciones originales e inspiradas.

J. Banks Design Group

SOUTH CAROLINA

Above: Because of the conservatory's gracious volume and inherent abundance of natural light, our primary challenges were designing appropriately scaled pieces and developing a color palette that wouldn't get washed out at the brightest times of day. We designed the soft blue and cream rug with a swirling pattern to give the room a sense of movement; we counterbalanced the light and airy piece with the coffee table, a large square upholstered in chocolate brown leather.

Facing Page Top & Bottom: We created a comfortable ambience with a twist for clients who were accustomed to traditional décor but desired something with a subtle contemporary edge. We found balance in style as well as texture and tone. In the kitchen, the cool metal juxtaposed with the rawness of the wood countertop creates a brilliant effect. Wood performs as a focal point in the living room, giving the eye a resting place from the expansive views of the garden. The natural palette connects the interior with nature but more importantly, draws attention to the homeowners' whimsical works of art.

Previous Page: Many of the pieces in our furniture line are named after members of our design team. High-backed chairs are somewhat of a signature for us—it's an Italian idea that we've brought to the States and has really caught on. Voluminous spaces need furniture tall enough to prevent it from getting lost—the high backs are also quite luxurious. The handles makes repositioning the chairs a breeze, so they're functional as well as aesthetically intriguing. Our furniture—chairs, tables and everything else—is available in a variety of finishes and is primarily transitional in style, so it works well in virtually every setting.

Photographs courtesy of J. Banks Design Group

"When you love what you do, challenges become opportunities."

—Joni Vanderslice

Above: For a home with a really open layout, we wanted to make a cozy dining area. We achieved this effect through bold yet complementary patterns, varying shades of green and brown, textures from velvet to wool and the high-backed banquette we designed to warmly envelop the residents as they dine. The banquette is a strong piece in the setting for its strength and intrigue—it's like a contemporized reproduction. It might seem like the rug was our inspiration for the room, but we actually came across it when the design was nearly complete—serendipitous things like this happen all the time for us because we have a large design team, always on the lookout for great pieces for each other's projects. With commissions across the country, we can cover a lot of ground fast. The chandelier was a New York find; we added the fringe for uniqueness.

Facing Page Top: We wanted to make the ski-in, ski-out space feel like a European lodge with a Western twist. The iron chandelier was made by a local artisan, and we had the hammered copper mantelpiece custom fabricated to add strength to the setting. The chairs were great antique market finds; we brought them back from London and had them reupholstered in cut-velvet to juxtapose the red leather sofa. After a day on the snow-covered Rockies, people love lounging fireside, playing chess by the window or relaxing in one of the numerous other seating nooks.

Facing Page Bottom: Untraditional fabrics really accentuate the bold lines of our furniture designs. We spend a lot of time perfecting nailhead details on chairs, ottomans and whatever else needs a special touch. The white lacquered mirror is from our extensive wall décor collection.

Photographs courtesy of J. Banks Design Group

"Design doesn't have to be complicated."
—Joni Vanderslice

Top: The fabric on the banquette was inspired by a tiny detail that we fell in love with; we enlarged the motif quite significantly and made the repetition irregular. The banquette is big and the print needed to hold its own so the whole piece doesn't fade into the background.

Bottom: We were commissioned to design the interiors of a series of historic farmhouses in the Italian countryside and used a number of local artisans and vendors. The blue and brown chest came from a local market; the urn in the courtyard was originally crafted as an olive oil jar. Whether or not we're designing in Europe, we infuse a lot of our work with an Italian feeling because it's just so warm and appealing.

Facing Page Top & Bottom: Villa Esperanza in Cabo San Lucas is an incredible property; its close proximity to the water and doors that fold all the way into the wall begged for a design with a distinct indoor-outdoor theme. The palapa ceiling treatment and imposing trusses enhance the connection, as do the natural colors, textures and fluid layout. We were involved with the architect early on in the project, so the architecture and interiors really function as one—the residents enjoy the large dining area and how it flows to the terrace. The bar, handcarved by a local cabinetmaker, definitely served as an inspiration piece; the mantelpiece nicely complements it, and we brought in the Mexican pottery and artwork for their organic forms and rich color and to further the relaxed, coastal ambience.

Photographs courtesy of J. Banks Design Group

" Juxtaposing old pieces with new designs is a great way to create warmth and authenticity."
—Joni Vanderslice

Robin Rains knows the profound effect our surroundings have on us—that the power of good design transforms our lives. These beliefs are what keep Robin and her Nashville-based boutique firm fervently committed to creating unique and influential interiors. With projects that span the United States, Robin's reputation has helped build an enthusiastic clientele. The combination of classic and timeless design adorned with the unexpected are characteristics of a Robin Rains Interior Design space. Though many of her projects are renovations, Robin prefers the totality of early involvement during the construction and design phase. She creates interiors to evoke an emotional response and complement a lifestyle, not dictate one. Robin's design inspiration comes in many forms—the 17th and 18th centuries, the colors and textures of nature, scale and proportion, and well-informed antiques. Helping to further supplement her passion for buying antiques, Robin intertwines her design business with her antique store, Old Hillsboro Antiques, located in historic Leiper's Fork.

Robin Rains a conscience de l'effet profond de notre environnement sur nous et sait qu'un décor bien composé a le pouvoir de transformer nos vies. Ce sont ces convictions qui expliquent l'engagement fervent et constant de Robin et de sa société et boutique de Nashville en faveur de la création d'intérieurs uniques et influents. Acquise dans le cadre de projets dans l'ensemble des États-Unis, la réputation de Robin lui vaut une clientèle enthousiaste. L'association de compositions classiques et intemporelles agrémentées d'inattendu caractérise les espaces décorés par Robin Rains Interior Design. Même si beaucoup de ses projets correspondent à des rénovations, Robin préfère être impliquée dès les premières phases de la construction et de la conception de l'ensemble d'un projet. Elle crée des intérieurs qui suscitent une réponse affective et complètent un style de vie, sans l'imposer. L'inspiration des créations de Robin prend de nombreuse formes : les 17e et 18e siècles, les couleurs et textures de la nature, l'échelle et les proportions, et les antiquités bien choisies. Le magasin d'antiquités de Robin, Old Hillsboro Antiques, dans la région historique de Leiper's Fork, lui permet également de s'adonner à sa passion pour les achats d'antiquités.

Robin Rains es conciente del efecto profundo que tiene el entorno sobre las personas y sabe que el buen diseño tiene la capacidad de transformar nuestras vidas. Dichas creencias son las que mantienen firme el compromiso de Robin y su compañía boutique con sede en Nashville en la creación de interiores únicos y significativos. Con proyectos a lo ancho de los Estados Unidos, la reputación de Robin le ha permitido hacerse de una clientela entusiasta. La combinación de diseño clásico y atemporal, adornado con toques inesperados constituyen las características de un espacio de Robin Rains Interior Design. A pesar de que muchos de sus proyectos son remodelaciones, Robin prefiere involucrarse al inicio del proyecto, durante la fase de construcción y diseño. Crea interiores para evocar una respuesta emocional y complementar un estilo de vida, en lugar de determinarlo. La inspiración de los diseños de Robin tiene diversas formas; los siglos XVII y XVIII, los colores y las texturas de la naturaleza, escala y proporción y las antigüedades. Para contribuir a su pasión por la compra de antigüedades, Robin combina su negocio de diseño con su tienda de antigüedades, Old Hillsboro Antiques, ubicada en el histórico Leiper's Fork.

Robin Rains

TENNESSEE

Above: The antique Biedermeier end table and custom-made walnut cocktail tables are complemented by neutral luxurious fabrics and beautiful clean lines. The custom sofa is upholstered in a Romo linen fabric with velvet pillows by Clarence House. An oversized antique four-panel Asian screen crafted of handpainted ink on teapaper gives the space drama. A collection of antique Chinese lacquered and jewel-inlaid calligraphy brushes with custom acrylic stands are displayed on the side table.
Photograph by Jerry Atnip

Facing Page Top: The New York City penthouse has sweeping views of Central Park, Lincoln Center and Columbus Avenue, so I designed the living room in a neutral palette—with accents of striking color to break up the monochromatic scheme—which directs the eye toward the window. Sophisticated and contemporary styles mix with exceptional antiques and custom pieces.
Photograph © Tim Lee Photography

Facing Page Bottom: The entry hall of a New York City penthouse introduces a neutral palette. Two striking elements inspire the design of the room: a wonderful 20th-century wooden pendant and the antique Biedermeier secretary. We designed the Art-Deco-style settee and custom made it for the space. The hanging mixed media metal sculpture is by Anton Weiss.
Photograph © Tim Lee Photography

Previous Page: The fluidity of the staircase echoes the grandeur of the colonnade with its groin-vaulted ceiling. I found the large, rare collection of late 18th-century exterior engravings and interior floorplans of English country houses in the neoclassic style. The center table has an old painted pedestal with a striking inlaid marquetry top and holds the soulful sculpture titled *Contrition*, a limited edition bronze by Clay Enoch.
Photograph by Jerry Atnip

Above: Imagine each morning spent in a light-filled, calming breakfast room. A custom banquette was fabricated and upholstered in Roger Arlington fabric with Ultrasuede bolsters. After searching months for the perfect dining table, I found a very old and rare late 17th-century Italian trestle table with the original painted finish. Not only was the size perfect, but the gold color with black accents and original ironwork could not have worked more brilliantly in the white, black and chrome eclectic breakfast room; it was the antique we needed to complement the custom banquette. Slip-covered dining chairs were placed on casters for ease of movement. The mix of vintage club chairs with black painted frames and Art Deco lounge chairs gives the space further interest. I bought the large mirror in Paris—it was fabricated from an exterior window pediment from a circa 1880 church. It adds a wonderful architectural element to the space and still has the original paint. The pair of antique pine columns were "found" objects purchased in New England.

Facing Page Top: We designed the library to have a warm Old World, comfortable elegance. The paneled oak walls are waxed to give a warm, aged appearance. The room is filled with inimitable, special pieces that make you want to linger in the space. The French Art Deco cocktail table features inlay of burl, satinwood and Macassar ebony. We chose an Art Deco-style table as we wanted to mix in some contemporary elements with our antiques, one of which is the circa 1900 Turkish Oushak rug selected from Bradford's. The charming Louis XIV 17th-century armchair, covered in hand-tooled gold damask leather reinforces the Old World effect.

Facing Page Bottom: We created a gentlemen's master retreat that had to be tailored, masculine and sophisticated yet would incorporate light tones. We chose hues of grays and whites with accents of cinnamon for our color palette. Donghia wool fabric drapery panels create a separation between the sleeping area and the lounging area.
Photographs by Jerry Atnip

Top: The custom sofa we designed and had Stewart Furniture produce is located just off a billiards room within a home's bar lounge. I feel that *Steam Train* by Chattanooga artist Scott Hill, adds a theme of progress encompassed by nostalgia to the room—a thought provoking piece of artwork, it is a conversation starter. The sofa, of linen velvet fabric by Pollack and throw pillows by Donghia, has a very tall back and resembles something that might have been found in a 1920s' European train station.

Center: A master bath has his-and-hers custom-made matching vanities, which are stained black to complement the gray and beige travertine top. Unusual custom mirrors of hand-forged iron suspend in a cut-out space leading to the master hallway.

Bottom: The design element of a living room began around an 18th-century wood-carved chandelier from Normandy. One of my favorite pieces, and one that makes the room so special, is the one-of-a-kind, oversized 19th-century carved wood mirror I purchased in France. This was the second home I created for these clients, so I knew their taste and they trusted my work. They wanted a beautiful room for entertaining guests after long days on the golf course, therefore, we decided on a palette of cool tones.

Facing Page: A salon is a must for those who love entertaining. Knowing the intent for the space, we gave a lot of thought to the flow and arrangement of each area within the expansive room. A neutral palette simply glows with strategically placed lighting, which allows the true value of the room's amazing architecture to really shine. The fine built elements of the room are a beautiful stage for classic design as well as the carefully selected antiques and furnishings. As the focal point of the room the limestone mantel was chipped and tea-stained to give an aged appearance. We used Peacock Pavers to resemble old stone floors, Venetian plaster gives a well-worn Italian flavor and the rich detail of the coffered ceiling adds aesthetic impact. I discovered the wonderful pair of Empire-style iron chandeliers with gilt metal beads in Europe. The antique pieces mixed with beautiful fabrics look collected, not decorated, and add to the timeless look. I love that this salon could as easily be found in a European home as one in the United States.
Photographs by Jerry Atnip

A very diverse group, Schelfe and Associates is attuned to holistic interior design. Always striving to encompass the whole of interior design, this eight-person team is headed by Tim Schelfe, President of the ASID Carolinas Chapter. Though Tim has made Raleigh his home, he has left his mark on the interiors of many residential and hospitality projects up and down the East Coast. His remarkable portfolio is a catalog for a lifetime of spatial consciousness, wherein the spaces we reside can shape our lives. Winner of multiple design awards, and featured in numerous design publications, Schelfe and Associates seeks to improve the quality of life for its clients through exceptional interior design.

Schelfe and Associates, un groupe très divers, est à l'écoute de l'architecture d'intérieur holistique. Cette équipe de huit personnes s'efforce toujours d'incorporer toutes les dimensions de la décoration intérieure, sous la direction de Tim Schelfe, Président du chapitre des Carolines de l'ASID. Même si Tim a élu résidence à Raleigh, il a laissé sa marque sur les intérieurs de nombreux projets résidentiels et hôteliers sur toute la Côte Est. Son portefeuille remarquable témoigne d'une vie caractérisée par une conscience spatiale élevée, dans laquelle les espaces dans lesquels nous vivons peuvent façonner nos vies. Lauréats de plusieurs prix dans le domaine du design, ayant fait l'objet d'articles dans de nombreuses publications, Schelfe and Associates entend améliorer la qualité de la vie de ses clients par une décoration intérieure exceptionnelle.

Schelfe and Associates constituye un grupo muy diverso, dedicado al diseño de interiores holístico. Constantemente en la búsqueda de abarcar la totalidad del diseño de interiores, este equipo de ocho personas está liderado por Tim Schelfe, el presidente de la delegación de las Carolinas de la Asociación de Decoradores de Interiores de EEUU (ASID, por sus siglas en inglés). A pesar de que Tim ha convertido a la ciudad de Raleigh en su hogar, ha dejado su marca en los interiores de muchos proyectos residenciales y de hospitalidad en toda la costa este de EEUU. Su extraordinaria cartera de clientes constituye un catálogo para toda una vida de conciencia espacial, según la cual los espacios en los que residimos pueden determinar nuestras vidas. Ganadores de varios premios de diseño y presentados en numerosas publicaciones de la actividad, Schelfe and Associates buscan mejorar la calidad de vida de sus clientes a través de un diseño de interiores excepcional.

Tim Schelfe

NORTH CAROLINA

Photograph by Jerry Blow

Above: Oftentimes, homeowners who have traditional exteriors will turn to the eclectic for the interior. French doors open to a rich layering of draperies—the bronze tone mimicked in the glazed accent dots and glass tile mosaic border within the Crema Marfil marble tile. The owner's aesthetic is truly reflected: A love of purple begat the chairs, while the light fixture and Sinatra-Minnelli painting came from the owner's collection.
Photograph by Jerry Blow

Right: Dark cherry cabinets are flush veneer so that the grain moves consistently across the room. Stainless steel tubular hardware mirrors the appliances. The dining room's glass mosaic floor tiles make another appearance as the kitchen's wall covering, giving a great sparkle to a magnetic room.
Photograph by Jerry Blow

Facing Page: We set the stage for drama. A soft, upholstered lambrequin glamorizes the window treatment, while the glass-beaded wall covering offers that Golden Age drama, likening the age of *Casablanca*. Oversized lamps purposely offset the size of the lambrequin. Giving weight to the corner, a blue sapphire chair shows the finale for an evening's cocktail party—a place to rest the couture black dress.
Photographs by Dustin Peck

Previous Page: The master suite of the 2008 ASID Carolinas Designer Showhouse design was derived from two fine jewelry photographs: Diamond jewelry sat against a clean white background, accented by deep blue sapphires. Different tones of white meet the blue accents, while the chandelier, wall sconces and crystal curtain trim glitter like diamonds.
Photograph by Dustin Peck

Above & Left: A remodeling project turned a 1920s' historic home into a modern arts room. A heavy brass chandelier was replaced by a low-voltage, paper-shade light fixture for whimsy. The khaki wall covering blends smoothly with the monochromatic cream and the chocolate accents. Notice the curvature of the furniture; conversations seem to flow with greater ease around soft corners. A bronze tabletop sculpture and an Art Nouveau corner piece give an ethereal air to the room, while balancing the classical lines of the baby grand piano.
Photographs by Seth Tice Lewis

Facing Page Top: We designed the entirety of the French Country home. From construction to moulding to finishes—a seamless integration of architecture and interior design is achieved. The ceiling is a plane that is often ignored. The panels of the coffered ceiling were tinted to offset the cream coloring. The living room fireplace anchors the space and is flanked by painted bookcases.
Photograph by Jerry Blow

Facing Page Bottom: The simple bones of a classic, clean kitchen meet professional quality and stainless steel appliances. The custom cabinetry is a cool cream, while the natural granite countertops offer warmth and practicality. Natural light pours in abundance, making the fresh and bright kitchen the envy of any French chef.
Photograph by Jerry Blow

"Great design will often stir your central core."
—Tim Schelfe

Top: Art imitates life; above the buffet, peeking beyond the white Dutch tulips, is the serene beauty of a koi pond painting.

Center: The powder room is a great opportunity to utilize a unique piece of furniture, transforming it into an elegant vanity with custom, polished black marble.

Bottom: The library windows flank a built-in bookcase to create a cozy and comfortable reading space. I could read and relax all day long in the plush chair.

Facing Page: The custom fireplace mantelpiece is hand-carved cherry, which came from the client's source—a testament to the tailoring involved in interior design: I may design a home and its interior, but the owner will always be the occupant!
Photographs by Jerry Blow

Basic instincts have never been good enough for Stan Topol. A student of the revered Billy Baldwin, the supposed dean of American interior design, Stan has spent a career developing a natural inclination for design into a highly refined gift. He rooted himself in Atlanta, where he founded his namesake firm, Stan Topol & Associates. For some 30 years, perfect spaces have been created under his hand; these homes grow and develop alongside the homeowners because of the discovery of the self in each project. Stan has a national reputation for stylish, controlled design based on a wealth of education in the field. And to quote Stan, "Having style does not mean one has to be stylish," and he lives by these words.

L'instinct de base n'a jamais été suffisant pour Stan Topol. Élève du grand Billy Baldwin et probablement doyen de la décoration intérieure américaine, Stan a consacré sa carrière à faire de son inclinaison naturelle pour la décoration un don hautement raffiné. Il s'est installé à Atlanta, où il a fondé la société qui porte son nom, Stan Topol & Associates. Depuis quelques 30 ans, il crée des espaces parfaits. Ses maisons croissent et se développement avec leurs propriétaires qui se découvrent dans chaque projet. Stan est réputé dans tout le pays pour ses créations élégantes et maîtrisées, qui prennent leurs sources dans sa connaissance approfondie de son domaine. Pour citer Stan, « Avoir du style n'est pas synonyme d'être à la mode », un principe qu'il met en pratique.

Los instintos básicos nunca han resultado suficientemente buenos para Stan Topol. Un estudiante del reverenciado Billy Baldwin, el supuesto decano del diseño de interiores de EEUU, Stan dedicó su carrera a convertir una inclinación natural por el diseño en un don altamente refinado. Se radicó en Atlanta, donde fundó la compañía que lleva su nombre, Stan Topol & Associates. Durante aproximadamente 30 años fue responsable de la creación de espacios perfectos; dichos hogares crecen y se desarrollan junto a sus propietarios, debido al descubrimiento de cada uno de ellos en cada proyecto. Stan cuenta con una reputación a nivel nacional de un diseño elegante y controlado, basado en una rica educación en el área. En sus propias palabras, "tener estilo no significa ser elegante», principio que sigue al pie de la letra.

Stan Topol

GEORGIA

Above: For the sitting room, we avoided anything trendy by underplaying nature and keeping to earth tones. Setting the period are a wonderful pair of chairs from the 1930s and velvet drapes. The quiet palette draws the eye to a great abstract wall piece.
Photograph by Brian Gassel

Facing Page Top: One of the most beautiful master baths that we've created was based on a clever separation of wet and dry, stretching out compartmentalized spaces—everything has a place. Smart clients draw out the best in me, and this client asked me to take the design all the way.
Photograph by Lynn McGill for Menefee + Winer Architects

Facing Page Bottom: Versatility is a must. The owner's style is what you see, for her art collection needed to honor the architecture. We bring the art into focus by understating the furniture: The leather-covered coffee table is a hushed piece amid such strong reds. It was created in Paris for the room more than 10 years ago.
Photograph by Brian Gassel

Previous Page: Corridors should always be a part of the flow of the house from inside to out. We took a smooth direction: Leading to the loggia and the pool, the corridor is about accessibility, and we used an antique Italian chest with the client's pottery to reinforce this. Therefore, the corridor becomes a room in itself.
Photograph by Tre Dunham, Fine Focus Photography

Above: When the client moved out of her bigger home, she wanted to inventory her pieces—keeping only the best. We dressed the interiors to the woman. The paintings, the pottery and the rococo chairs all reflect a woman with remarkable style.
Photograph by Mali Azima

Left: A collection of Chinese pottery, contemporary rock crystal shapes, a coromandel screen and Rose Tarlow chairs meet in a comfortable reading corner.
Photograph by Mali Azima

Facing Page Top: Developed around the opposing, elegant painting, the room is an exploration in serenity and calm.
Photograph by Mali Azima

Facing Page Bottom: The entire Utah home was a piece of art, from which the bedroom stemmed. Everything started from the arrangement of furniture, which is why all of my projects are hand drawn at conception—to define the space absolutely.
Photograph by alanblakely.com

"Houses need to grow with you, to
develop with you. Personal style, as a
result, is everything."

—Stan Topol

Right: An eclectic corner features several wonderful pieces. Most impressive is the console discovered by the client himself. The project turned out marvelously because of it.

Facing Page: At the top of a modern building sits a tremendous apartment—it was the project of a lifetime. Dark woods pull you through the arched entries into the cavernous living room. Cindy Kirkland did the detailing here, while the furniture—chairs from Rose Tarlow—sits beneath antique chandeliers.
Photographs by Bill LaFevor

"Basic instincts are not good enough for me. Education in the field—developing the knack—can turn a vision into a truth."
—Stan Topol

Three to four times a year Carole Weaks revisits France, a country known for its commitment to elemental beauty—from food and wine to art. France has served to renew her design perspectives over the past two decades. Interspersed among her residential designs are the treasures she finds from French and American showrooms and artists, many of whom she has consistently followed over the years observing their creative patterns. With this knowledge and experience, Carole offers her clients myriad perspectives and often swings open a door to design possibilities they never knew existed. Understanding that art must never be rushed, she does not push clients into hasty purchases. It is this outlook and her steady approach to design that guide each home to reflect a new facet of beauty.

Trois à quatre fois par an, Carole Weaks repart en France, un pays réputé pour son engagement en faveur de la beauté élémentaire, de la nourriture au vin, en passant par l'art. La France lui a permis de renouveler ses perspectives créatives tout au long des vingt dernières années. Les trésors qu'elle trouve dans les salons d'exposition et chez les artistes français et américains, dont elle suit beaucoup depuis des années en observant leurs compositions créatives, parsèment ses créations résidentielles. Grâce à ses connaissances et son expérience, Carole permet à ses clients de bénéficier d'une myriade de perspectives et ouvre souvent la porte à des possibilités de création dont ils n'auraient jamais eu conscience. Elle sait que l'art ne doit jamais être hâté et n'incite pas ses clients à prendre des décisions d'achat trop rapidement. C'est cette perspective et son approche cohérente de la décoration qui régissent son aménagement de chaque maison pour en faire le reflet d'une nouvelle facette de la beauté.

Carole Weaks visita Francia tres o cuatro veces al año, un país reconocido por su dedicación a la belleza elemental, para disfrutar desde su comida, de sus vinos y de su arte. Durante las últimas dos décadas, Francia ha contribuido a renovar sus perspectivas de diseño. Mezclados con sus diseños residenciales se encuentran los tesoros que encuentra en muestras y artistas franceses y norteamericanos, muchos de los cuales ha seguido consistentemente durante años observando sus patrones creativos. Con tal conocimiento y experiencia, Carole ofrece a sus clientes una miríada de perspectivas y a menudo pone a su disposición posibilidades de diseño que jamás imaginaron. Convencida de que nunca se debe apresurar el arte, no presiona a sus clientes para concretar compras apresuradas. La guía para que cada hogar refleje una nueva faceta de belleza la constituye justamente esta perspectiva y su firme enfoque al diseño.

Carole Weaks
GEORGIA

Above, Facing Page Top & Previous Page: Several years earlier, I had designed my clients' living room in a pleasant mixture of yellow and other colors. It was a strong combination and since the couple loves redecorating, they decided to explore new design possibilities. With friendly fabrics, an art piece above the fireplace by Mark Webber with just a hint of yellow and French furniture, we developed a completely different ambience for the room. Set before the couch is a pair of garden stools whose unusual tops happened to reflect all the colors within the fabric—if they had been white, the impact would have been lessened drastically. The kitchen was also completely renovated to include a bar, more work space, and two chandeliers above the island.
Photographs by Chris Little

Facing Page Bottom: Pastel and charcoal drawings serve as the perfect balance to the master bedroom's French blue walls. I chose that particular shade of blue because its depth and interest keeps the room from being boring. A French chair is covered in Zimmer Rodhe cut velvet; the nightstand is actually one of a pair of bronze and glass consoles that I purchased while in France.
Photograph by Erica George-Dines Photography

"The beauty of design is its continual development—there is always something to refine."

—Carole Weaks

Above & Facing Page Top: I was given the opportunity to design the main living space for the 2006 Atlanta Symphony Showhouse, and there were several design challenges that had to be addressed. First, the enormity of the space was quite a challenge—it seemed to swallow furniture—so I divided the room into three different areas. Within a typical residence, rarely are all the rooms occupied throughout an entire day. But the showhouse had to function with constant visitors during both day and nighttime presentations. In such a large room, it's not pleasant to see dramatic bunches of color spread out across the space, so I incorporated neutral fabrics, harmonious wall colors and draperies, allowing the space to transition with the natural light. French antique bookcases add definition to the walls, while the French antique chaise and canapé are covered in contemporary fabrics. A touch of orange via pillows and subtle accessories works well with both day and night lighting.
Photographs by Emily Followill

Right: What makes the room truly spectacular is its 1940s' Jansen desk. The unusual curvature of the piece with its leather top with steel and bronze fittings makes it a magnificent addition to the 2008 Atlanta Symphony Showhouse. John Hyche painted the bright art piece resting above the fireplace.
Photograph by Chris Little

Facing Page Bottom: As is typical among homes in Atlanta's Buckhead neighborhood built in the 1940s, the home neither had large rooms nor extremely ornate architectural details, so to accommodate this straightforward style, I bought a modestly sized French chandelier to place in the dining room. Resting above an 18th-century commode is a piece from a French artist.
Photograph by Erica George-Dines Photography

Top: One of the largest rooms I've ever worked with was a bedroom inside the 2008 Atlanta Symphony Showhouse. Its size required extremely careful consideration of material choices. Using a pewter grasscloth wall covering gave the room a wonderful texture, which helped diminish the cavernous feel of the space. The bed was custom designed to bring more activity to the room—a wooden bed wouldn't have filled the space sufficiently—and the drawings above the bed were acquired from one of my favorite young artists in France. In certain parts of the room, a pretty blush tone was used to give a subtle coloration and warmth. We were actually a little nervous about using that shade because if there happened to be too much, the room would have felt contrived. In the end it was such a nice color and it came together quite well.
Photograph by Chris Little

Bottom: To give the living room versatility, the corner is arranged with a game table, a banquette and three chairs. Not only can it be used for conversation, but it also serves as an excellent area for additional guest seating at a dinner party or a more intimate dining venue.
Photograph by Erica George Dines Photography

Facing Page Top: Because the home had many rooms, we had the luxury of designating the study as an adult retreat. While there is quite a bit of antique furniture, I used a Lucite and glass table to mix things up a little bit. The draperies are a stronger color than I normally select, but the soft, burnished red works well with the space.
Photograph by Deborah Whitlaw Llewellyn

Facing Page Bottom Left: Just off the barreled ceiling foyer with chandeliers and custom wallpaper by Arena Design, the formal living room is handsomely decorated with a painted French chair and sophisticated furniture selections.
Photograph by Deborah Whitlaw Llewellyn

Facing Page Bottom Right: The sitting room's neutral taupe background complements the gray Zoffany fabric on the couch. Reflected within the art and cut velvet fabric is a delicate portion of melon and deep red tones.
Photograph by Erica George Dines Photography

"A little of a good thing is sometimes exactly what you need!"

—Carole Weaks

Interior design, in a way, is a kind of dance; there is a personal expression being made to flow throughout a home. Douglas Weiss—a native of Vancouver—spent his early years as a professional ballet dancer. Dance and theater are communicative arts, and so when Doug retired from ballet, he redirected his innate penchant for the expressive to interior design—a lifelong interest of his. Douglas Weiss Interiors is a way for Doug to feed his passion, which is to create wonderfully unique spaces for interesting people. By finding the personal expressions of his clients, Doug becomes the raconteur of the home's narrative.

La décoration intérieure est une sorte de danse. Il s'agit d'une expression personnelle qui circule dans l'ensemble d'une maison. Douglas Weiss — originaire de Vancouver — a commencé sa carrière comme danseur classique professionnel. La danse et le théâtre sont des arts de la communication, de sorte que lorsque Doug a mis fin à sa carrière de danseur, il a redirigé son goût inné de l'expression vers la décoration intérieure, qui l'avait toujours intéressé. Douglas Weiss Interiors est pour Doug une façon d'exprimer sa passion, qui consiste à créer des espaces magnifiquement uniques pour des gens intéressants. En déchiffrant les expressions personnelles de ses clients, Doug se fait le conteur de l'histoire de la maison.

De alguna manera, el diseño de interiores constituye una forma de danza; se da una expresión personal que fluye a través de todo el hogar. Douglas Weiss, un nativo de Vancouver, dedicó los primeros años de su vida a la danza profesional de ballet. La danza y el teatro constituyen artes comunicativos, de manera que cuando Doug se retiró del ballet, redirigió su pasión innata por lo expresivo hacia el diseño de interiores, su interés de toda la vida. Para Doug, Douglas Weiss Interiors constituye una manera de satisfacer su pasión, crear espacios maravillosamente exclusivos para personas interesantes. Al descubrir las expresiones personales de sus clientes, Doug se convierte en el cronista de la narrativa del hogar.

Douglas Weiss

Above Left: Paler tones meet deep black and red hues. I commissioned the artwork specifically for the homeowner. The art adds flavor and personality for a client who is new to collecting.

Above Right: The color scheme flows throughout the home. The living room is based on symmetrical arrangements, with pairs of sofas and tables. Metallic tones—gold, bronze and copper—combine with Venetian plaster walls for a textural experience.

Facing Page: The whole house played with different shades of reds and neutrals, accented in the master bedroom with blacks. The hand-wrought iron bench with rolled cover and the bamboo-post bed deliver a unique graphic effect.

Previous Page: A lot of inspiration comes from the architecture. The mahogany panels demand a palette that works well with the tone of the wood. Custom furniture is balanced with the pale rug—the terracotta fabric and green of the marble are a nice punch. But the focal point of the room—and the embodiment of the color scheme—is the great abstract painting.
Photographs by Erica George Dines Photography

" I always encourage homeowners to have a conscious style. Finding their lifestyles means everything."

—Douglas Weiss

" A lot of design is about balancing masculine and feminine—choosing handsome or beautiful."

—Douglas Weiss

Left & Facing Page: My own home was built in 1908. I designed the dining room around the antique Amari porcelain pieces. I think the details have to be tailored to the room, have to be very definitive. The upholstered Klismos-style chairs hug the sitter with perfect comfort. The chandelier incorporates the Greek key to pair with the chairs. I used a leopard print rug for neutrality, but you have to be careful—you don't want to overdo it. The reflected painting was commissioned and is a take on the old Rock, Paper, Scissors game—very allegorical, which is a great focal point for the room and a perfect foil for dining room conversation.
Photographs by Erica George Dines Photography

"We all have a storytelling nature, and the home should represent that."

—Douglas Weiss

Top: Charleston-style windows offer wonderful natural light for the study off the master bedroom. The handblocked linen curtains are light and beautiful. A custom-designed rug grounds the room by providing movement through its pattern. The abstract painting is placed to mimic a design element in the curtains.

Center: Geared to the lady of the house, the room is more feminine. The art squares are of encaustic wax, not of certain colors, but rather blocks of layers of colors, related but not matching.

Bottom: The furniture is very continental, but the antique writing desk gives an Italian flavor. Beyond the desk is a great abstract painting, botanical and very expressive.

Facing Page: The showhouse library was all about color and shape. Geometric lines on the coffered ceiling—the rectilinear form—and the paneling contrast with softer, more inviting shapes, such as the circular alabaster chandelier, wall mirror and Chinese jade disks. I designed the rug after the quatrefoil, but gave the ancient shape a fresh look with its large scale and color. The rug also reflects the ceiling, but the color pulls you in.

Photographs by Erica George Dines Photography

From an early age Charles Allem loved design and knew he had a passion for creating luxurious, inviting and timeless spaces. At the young age of 20 Charles was already running one of the premier design studios in his native South Africa. In 1988 he began his own firm in California and over the years has transitioned his company into its current format, CAD International, which undertakes commercial and residential commissions around the world of varying scale, scope and nature. Charles' design aesthetic is one of strength, discipline and balance and he considers interior and exterior architecture in concert, working simultaneously from the inside out and the outside in. Constantly seeking new and exciting challenges, Charles maintains he is still savoring the incredible journey that began years ago in Johannesburg.

Dès un âge précoce, Charles Allem aimait dessiner et avait conscience de sa passion pour la création d'espaces de luxe accueillants et intemporels. Au jeune âge de 20 ans, Charles dirigeait déjà un des plus grands studios de création de l'Afrique du Sud dont il est originaire. En 1988, il a lancé sa propre société en Californie et l'a transformée au cours des ans pour lui donner son format actuel, CAD International, qui se voit confier des projets commerciaux et résidentiels d'échelles, de magnitudes et de natures variées dans le monde entier. L'esthétique des créations de Charles est caractérisée par sa force, sa discipline et son équilibre. Il aborde l'architecture intérieure et extérieure ensemble, et travaille simultanément de l'intérieur vers l'extérieur et de l'extérieur vers l'intérieur. Toujours à la recherche de défis nouveaux et stimulants, Charles avoue toujours savourer l'incroyable voyage qui a commencé il y a des années à Johannesbourg.

Desde una edad muy temprana, Charles Allem fue un enamorado del diseño y supo que su pasión era la creación de espacios lujosos, atractivos y atemporales. Con apenas 20 años, Charles ya dirigía uno de los principales estudios de diseño de su Sudáfrica natal. En 1988 fundó su propia compañía en California y, con los años, la llevó hacia el formato actual, CAD International, la que se dedica a proyectos comerciales y residenciales de diversas escalas, alcances y naturaleza en todo el mundo. La estética de diseño de Charles es sólida, disciplinada y balanceada y considera la arquitectura interior y exterior en conjunto, trabajando simultáneamente desde adentro hacia fuera y desde afuera hacia adentro. Constantemente buscando nuevos e interesantes desafíos, Charles sostiene que sigue disfrutando del increíble viaje que comenzó hace muchos años en Johannesburgo.

Charles Allem

Above: I love designing master suites to have wonderful privacy, and for a client in Los Angeles I gave great privacy yet took full advantage of the jaw-dropping panoramic views out to Malibu and Pasadena. The chocolate brown crocodile leather nightstand and dark walnut are the perfect complement to the palette's white and kelly green.
Photograph by John Ellis

Left: We purchased the vintage 1960s' chaise in New York and its leather is wonderful in the very textural living room, which includes suede, silk, stainless steel and walls in a high-gloss kelly green lacquer.
Photograph by John Ellis

Facing Page Top: A contemporary English library, the space features deep espresso brown walnut paneling and walls in a red lacquer. Great bones enabled us to design an iconic, masculine room with stainless steel staircase and balustrade; the desk and built-ins are all cantilevered.
Photograph by Everett Fenton Gidley

Facing Page Bottom: In my interiors I am very driven by art and architecture, and the Andy Warhol series of prints 'Flash' was ideal for the library; the custom staircase was forged on site.
Photograph by John Ellis

Previous Page: On what was originally a driveway we extended the porte cochere and created a monolithic stainless steel entry that opens electronically onto the street. A checkerboard of grass and poured white terrazzo flanks the entrance and leads to contemporary Italian gardens.
Photograph by John Ellis

"Editing and streamlining are every bit as important as buying and acquiring—spatial flow is the name of the game."

—Charles Allem

Top: I designed the staircase on a napkin as a piece of sculpture that connects the entire house from all different levels. It twists and turns up to a 14-foot organic pyramid capping the house, suffusing light all the way down into the core. It is truly an experience to walk though.
Photograph by Everett Fenton Gidley

Bottom: A signature piece by Daume rests at the bottom of the three-level staircase; a palette of amethyst and purple deviates from other levels and plays off the amethyst sculpture.
Photograph by Everett Fenton Gidley

Facing Page Top: A continuous wall of glass ensures utterly captivating views in a room of luxurious comfort. I covered the sofa, which came from Francis Ford Coppola's residence, in chocolate brown lambskin while the pillows and pair of 1950s' Rafael chairs are upholstered in kelly green sheared mink.
Photograph by John Ellis

Facing Page Bottom: Rather than a sleek, modern table we went for a more classic contemporary table, which seats six in custom chairs with apple green mohair; a splash of wheatgrass in the table's center provides a rich organic element. The picture is by Adam Fuss.
Photograph by John Ellis

"I approach each commission with an eye for creating something different and extraordinary yet that encompasses the lifestyle of the client, the location, nature and all the essential disciplines of design."

—Charles Allem

A background in art education certainly equipped Tim Bagwell for successful involvement with the world of interior design. His artistic eye is always ready to soak in new inspiration—even his drafted years in the U.S. Army and time spent as a NATO illustrator served his broad perspectives via European travel. Tim's intuitive sensibilities as the principal of T. Bagwell Interiors shine through his relationship-building skills, and have certainly paved the way for the many high-profile clientele who trust their homes and even corporate spaces to his design intelligence. Continually blessed with the opportunity to create engaging interiors of beauty and tranquility, Tim wakes up each day with a contagious energy and optimism that can't help but reflect in even the tiniest details.

Sa formation à l'enseignement de l'art a certainement préparé Tim Bagwell à une carrière réussie dans le monde de la décoration intérieure. Son sens artistique est toujours à la recherche d'une nouvelle source d'inspiration. Même ses années dans l'armée américaine et en tant qu'illustrateur pour l'OTAN ont contribué à élargir sa perspective par des voyages en Europe. Les sensibilités intuitives de Tim à la tête de T. Bagwell Interiors sont visibles dans ses compétences en matière de relations, et l'ont certainement préparé à servir la nombreuse clientèle de haut niveau qui confie à son intelligence créatrice sa maison et même des espaces d'entreprise. Tim, qui a la chance de disposer constamment d'opportunités de création d'intérieurs attrayants empreints de beauté et de tranquillité, se réveille tous les jours animé d'une énergie et d'un optimisme contagieux qui se traduisent immanquablement dans les détails les plus infimes.

Sin duda, una formación en educación artística brindó a Tim Bagwell las herramientas para involucrarse con éxito en el mundo del diseño de interiores. Su ojo artístico se encuentra siempre listo para absorber inspiraciones nuevas; aún sus años de servicio en el ejército de EEUU y el periodo en el que se desempeñó como ilustrador de la OTAN sirvieron para ampliar sus perspectivas a través de viajes por Europa. Sus sensibilidades intuitivas como director de T. Bagwell Interiors se reflejan a través de su habilidad para el desarrollo de relaciones y ciertamente han facilitado la adquisición de una amplia clientela de gran exposición, que confía sus hogares y hasta sus espacios corporativos a su inteligencia de diseño. Constantemente bendecido por la oportunidad de crear interiores atractivos de belleza y tranquilidad, Tim comienza cada día con una energía y optimismo contagioso que se refleja hasta en los detalles más insignificantes.

Tim Bagwell

NORTH CAROLINA

Above: When my clients returned from a family trip to South Africa, they brought with them a large zebra rug, which fit perfectly in the home's formal living room. To continue this theme in a more casual environment, I designed another living area with a similar motif. We brought in a zebra ottoman and used the zebra chairs—which also came from the homeowners' Africa travels—to complement the rain forest depiction on the walls. Adding to the detail of the room are a large wooden giraffe, a Masland area rug and cane sticks in the corner. Quite simply, the area successfully reflected the entire family's interests and experiences.

Facing Page Top: I derived inspiration for the formal drawing room from the Ertel print placed above the sofa. A yellow Damas sofa and custom Masland rug with a zebra border give the space a sophisticated touch. But the real star of the room is the chinoiserie gold and black lacquered secretary. Since the room was simple, the secretary was an excellent choice because it's anything but ordinary.

Facing Page Bottom: The opportunity to design a more modern space allowed me the chance to show my design versatility. The juxtaposition of contemporary elements and the stone fireplace, which inspired the room's colors, exemplifies a room with comfortable livability.

Previous Page: The room's strength is found in the combination of various pieces: a china display by Karges, a red Masland custom carpet and a glass etched door that leads to the wine cellar. A stunning complement to the area is its natural limestone floor that has been laid in a diagonal pattern. My faux artist painted the banister and risers to give the illusion of limestone, too—this attention to detail is a signature of my style: to incorporate elemental illusions to enhance each project.

Photographs by Pat Shanklin

"Creativity doesn't end with the design of the room, but rather it continues into the complete presentation of the space."

—Tim Bagwell

Top: With a stunning chandelier and complementary sconces reflected, the luxurious bathroom offers an elegant retreat for its homeowners. Orchids and plentiful natural light from surrounding windows give a warm and pleasant ambience.
Photograph by Pat Shanklin

Bottom: Working with the open floorplan and exposed cedar beams created quite a challenge for the 2008 March of Dimes home. With no separation between the gathering room, dining and kitchen areas, I designed a space that was large, open, but also inviting. I repeated the rustic feeling by including a cedar beam mantel and choosing knotty alder for the kitchen cabinets and built-ins, which provide other natural textures. Arranging the eight individually potted orchids in front of the farm sink at the window complete the coziness and understated elegance.
Photograph by Michael Valentine

Facing Page: Setting the stage for the grand salon is the magnificent view of the North Carolina towering pine trees and the sunset reflecting on the lake water. I thoroughly enjoyed the process of infusing an Old World ambience that contributes to the room's grandeur and its welcoming essence. The formal living space ushers guests into an evening of refined entertainment.
Photograph by Pat Shanklin

The single biggest influence in Robin Bergeson's life and work is her mother, a remarkable woman and artist. A love of art, acquired from her mother, antiques and collections, is a recurrent theme throughout her work. Traveling is another passion and the exposure to different cultures opens her eyes to many rich design possibilities. The principal of Bergeson Design Studio, Robin feels the design process should be a collaboration between client and designer and thoroughly enjoys working alongside clients to reach their design goals.

La mère de Robin Bergeson, une femme et artiste remarquable, est la personne qui à elle seule a influencé le plus sa vie. L'amour de l'art, qu'elle tient de sa mère, les antiquités et les collections, forment un thème récurrent que l'on retrouve dans l'ensemble de son œuvre. Le voyage est une autre de ses passions et l'exposition à différentes cultures lui ouvre les yeux à de nombreuses possibilités créatrices. Directrice de Bergeson Design Studio, Robin pense que le processus créatif doit être une collaboration entre le client et le décorateur. Elle apprécie pleinement le travail aux côtés des clients au service de leurs objectifs en matière de décoration.

La mayor influencia en la vida y obra de Robin Bergeson es su madre, una mujer y artista extraordinaria. El tema recurrente en toda su obra es su pasión por el arte, adquirido de su madre, las antigüedades y las colecciones. Otra de sus pasiones son los viajes y la exposición a culturas diferentes le permitió descubrir una enorme variedad de valiosas posibilidades de diseño. Robin, la directora de Bergeson Design Studio, sostiene que el proceso de diseño debe resultar de la cooperación entre el cliente y el diseñador, y disfruta enormemente de trabajar junto a los clientes para lograr sus objetivos de diseño.

Robin Bergeson

VIRGINIA

Above: The clients' love of nature and art inspired the living room. A painting by one of their favorite artists is placed over the mantel, and a second focal point is created by grouping together a collection of identically framed, antique, water bird book plates.

Facing Page Top: I responded to my clients' request for an interesting, unique space for family and friends by filling the magnificent space with many special finds, like the carved wood wall panel and art nouveau-inspired chairs. The walls are a textured plaster finish with warm undertones using window treatments that allow for the play of light and unobstructed views. Layers of lighting: natural, artificial and candlelight—allow the clients to create different moods for different times of the day and for entertaining.

Facing Page Bottom: I designed the space for a relaxing evening— no television, no computer, no phone, just an evening enjoying great conversation and a fine glass of wine with friends and family. I grouped together a few well-chosen conversation pieces: three starburst mirrors and three handpainted, framed, antique, medallion prints aimed at setting an interesting background for a memorable evening.

Previous Page: I commissioned the group of oil paintings inspired by my personal shell collection. The crisp, blue and white china and shell-covered dinner memento boxes for each guest create an elegant yet whimsical feeling. Faux shagreen walls complete the sea-inspired theme.
Photographs by Gwin Hunt

Top: A cherished watercolor portrait, a vision of me as a young woman painted by my artist mother, is the focus of the sitting room in my home. An antique Belgian chair, bought for a song and lovingly restored, blends with other art and antiques collected during my travels to form a haven for quiet contemplation.

Bottom: I consider function, comfort and livability as important as the aesthetic appeal. In the master suite I have given the very busy career couple a retreat of their own. To achieve this I used a restful blue and brown color palette, minimal accessories and soft details.

Facing Page: Using a stunning Jack Leonard Larson fabric for the row of pillows, an unexpected waterfall skirt on a leather sectional, and placing them against an antique tapestry—a special designer find—I created a sophisticated yet comfortable family room that is great for relaxing in front of the television, gazing into the fireplace or even a game of chess.
Photographs by Gwin Hunt

"Delicately balancing the old and new, using both contemporary and distinguished older pieces, creates an eclectic design aesthetic that is truly timeless."

—Robin Bergeson

Always in search of timelessness, Janet Bilotti designs homes by focusing on the distinct variables in each project: Scale and architecture are mutable, and thus the materials must conform. Janet founded Janet Bilotti Interiors in 1994 based on these principles. Located in Naples, Florida, this award-winning firm has a sweeping portfolio with projects that stretch across the globe. A JBI residential interior is enduring, appropriate and remarkably creative.

En quête constante de l'intemporel, Janet Bilotti conçoit des résidences en s'attachant plus particulièrement aux variables distinctives de chaque projet : l'échelle et l'architecture sont variables, de sorte que les matériaux doivent s'y conformer. Janet a fondé Janet Bilotti Interiors en 1994 sur la base de ces principes. Les projets de l'impressionnant portfolio de ce cabinet d'architecture primé situé à Naples, en Floride, couvrent le monde entier. Un intérieur résidentiel de JBI est durable, approprié et remarquablement créatif.

Siempre en la búsqueda de lo atemporal, Janet Bilotti diseña hogares poniendo énfasis en las variables distintivas de cada proyecto: La escala y la arquitectura son cambiantes y, por lo tanto, los materiales deben adaptarse. Janet fundó Janet Bilotti Interiors en 1994 en base a esos principios. Con sede en Naples, Florida, esta compañía, ganadora de numerosos premios, dispone de una amplia cartera de clientes con proyectos en todo el mundo. Un interior residencial de JBI es duradero, apropiado y extraordinariamente creativo.

Janet Bilotti

FLORIDA

"A well-designed entrance should introduce a feeling for the impending interior spaces."
—Janet Bilotti

Above: Overlooking the mangroves of the Gulf of Mexico, the living room is a practice in balancing the sheer volume of the space. Larger art pieces are juxtaposed with smaller works to relate the scale: The satinwood art wall ascends two levels, warming the room. A black leather rug anchors the opening between sofa and table pairs.

Facing Page: The original room had little niches flanking the granite fireplace. We took this space to the other side—for media purposes—and covered it with satinwood panels. The Holly Hunt bench pairs with the Michael Berman cocktail table for purity, nicely offset by the abstract wax painting.

Previous Page: Right off the elevator, one steps into the private foyer that is narrowly minimalist and very inviting. The satinwood panels create warmth. The custom door and handle pair nicely with the historic carpet and the Nancy Corzine bench. The refined painting gives a hint of the coming spaces.
Photographs by Troy Campbell

Top: A fan of rich leather, the client is a big player in the media industry. The fireplace's former niches were brought in here for media racks. The room is clearly designed for comfort.

Bottom: With an army of children and grandchildren around, having private spaces was very important. The master bedroom—with its fireplace, pair of sofas and Barbara Barry bench—is a perfect place to enjoy morning coffee before joining the rest of the family.

Facing Page Top & Bottom: Continuing the satinwood motif, a buffet lines the dining room. The recessed wall was a great spot for a colorful abstract. Instead of a chandelier, we used a ceiling drop to keep the lines, while the direct and indirect lighting creates interesting effects on the artwork, the customized table and the Dakota Jackson furniture.
Photographs by Troy Campbell

"Presenting a new visual concept to a potential client is always challenging. But that's the fun and creative part."

—Janet Bilotti

chapter three

chapitre trois

capítulo tres

Midwest

A cohesive team of architectural and interior design visionaries, Charles R. Stinson Architects and CRS Interiors compose spaces of integration, connection and balance. By honing energy from the home's site—and working in concert with nature by framing views, sun and shade—light is balanced through even the most intricate spaces. It is this reverence for such natural amenities and accommodation to the site's functionality that undoubtedly produce interiors where clients' hopes, individual visions and lifestyle needs are met. CRS Interiors is committed to actively researching products and practices that make a positive impact on the global community. With a foundation built upon swift and efficient collaboration, truth and faith are fostered between designer and client to produce homes in which everyone takes pride.

Charles R. Stinson Architects et CRS Interiors, une équipe cohésive d'architectes et décorateurs visionnaires, composent des espaces d'intégration, de connexion et d'équilibre. Grâce à la mise à profit de l'énergie de la maison et de son environnement naturel par le cadrage des panoramas, du soleil et de l'ombre, la lumière est équilibrée même dans les espaces les plus compliqués. C'est ce respect pour les conditions naturelles du site et l'adaptation aux fonctionnalités de celui-ci qui permettent sans aucun doute de créer des intérieurs correspondant aux attentes, à la vision et au style de vie des clients. CRS Interiors entend rechercher activement des produits et pratiques susceptibles d'avoir un impact positif sur la communauté mondiale. Une fondation édifiée sur la base d'une collaboration rapide et efficace permet d'instaurer confiance et foi entre architecte et client pour aménager des espaces qui font la fierté de tous.

Charles R. Stinson Architects y CRS Interiors, un sólido equipo de visionarios arquitectónicos y de diseño de interiores, componen espacios de integración, conexión y balance. Aprovechando la energía del terreno y trabajando en conjunto con la naturaleza mediante el encuadre de las vistas, del sol y la sombra, se logra un balance de la luz aún a través de los espacios más intrincados. Es justamente esa reverencia por las características naturales y adaptación a la funcionalidad del terreno que sin lugar a dudas produce interiores en los que se satisface las esperanzas, visiones individuales y necesidades de estilo de vida de los clientes. CRS Interiors tiene el compromiso de la búsqueda activa de productos y prácticas que tengan un impacto positivo en la comunidad global. Con una base firmemente apoyada sobre la colaboración rápida y eficiente, la verdad y la fe son estimuladas entre el diseñador y el cliente para producir hogares de los que todo el mundo puede sentirse orgulloso.

CRS Interiors

Above: To create a harmonious entertaining space, the Valcucine kitchen was built into the side of the room. It evolves beautifully into the dining and living rooms—and burnished concrete block fireplace that extends to the exterior—while taking advantage of the ribbon windows as well.

Facing Page: A continued effect within the great room was used in the bathroom's rift sawn oak floors. We really appreciated the contrast in the bathroom: A freestanding white tub by Wet is complemented by the dark walnut wood cabinets. The dramatic textures were subtly woven within the Venetian plaster and its waxed finish, peacefully engaging the eye; the glass shower and obscured windows flow as a natural part of the residence.

Previous Page: Looking at most of our designs, we mainly prefer to engage the playful side of life. But inside the Minneapolis home we chose a simple elegance that honored the modern design of the site. To impart warmth, we took advantage of the wetland and neighborhood views and used 10-foot windows on each end of the house. We oriented the house to its location and incorporated a thin strip of ribbon windows so the room remained open, offering a glimpse of what's occurring outside. In keeping with the subdued direction of the interiors, we used Holly Hunt furniture throughout.
Photographs by Peter Bastianelli-Kerze

"Pay attention to the energy of a room—if it's overdone or not quite complete, a synergy won't be found."

—Ruth Johnson

"Whether using texturized plaster or richly colored columns, a space can effortlessly feel modern and warm simultaneously."

—Charles Thiss

Right: With a splash of blue, wood bench, and the intersecting stone hearth and red fireplace upon bamboo floors, the area tells the story of our vision for the entire home. It is a composition of color and light and exudes the playfulness we love to work with. The various textures, colors and elements accurately combine the architect's vision and the client's lifestyle.

Facing Page Top: The client for a lakeside cottage was a single mom whose son was 10 years old. Naturally she wanted a relaxing retreat for herself, but also a place where her son and his friends could feel comfortable. We chose a very durable bamboo floor to complement the maple kitchen cabinets and accommodate the varieties of entertaining that would undoubtedly occur throughout the home, by the fireplace and amongst the deep blue chaise style sofas. The interior echoes full views of the lake and surrounding nature through the yellow-gold paint above the fireplace; a u-shaped form above the fireplace mimics exterior architectural details. Our clients wanted a happy house and that's what we delivered.

Facing Page Bottom: Taking advantage of a pleasant connectedness within the whole house, the formal entertaining areas join the dining room and beyond. We took cues from the lake when choosing the blue rug to define the eating space. Next to one of the tall windows we strategically placed a plush white chair that can spin around to face the lake for that ever-important cup of morning coffee.
Photographs by Peter Bastianelli-Kerze

"The less-is-more part of design must be approached with care. Every vase and finish should be thoughtfully considered so there's harmony and balance."

—Ruth Johnson

Top: An earth-friendly and modern Italian manufacturer, Valcucine, built the kitchen in the open floorplan. The kitchen bar is an element we use often with expansive homes like this one. It's a nice way to hide dishes and sinks so that guests don't readily see those items when entering the home; an intimacy can be felt in the space and a casual social area is also naturally incorporated into the kitchen.

Center: To make the bathroom feel like a retreat, we used a floating island and tobacco gold limestone; we referenced Italian design by placing large tiles on the floor and letting them ascend the wall in various sizes. Instead of using Deco tile, we wanted a richness that reflected our clients' Indian culture and decided to use earthy tones. We gladly found the balance between a traditional look and modern warmth.

Bottom & Facing Page: A young professional couple came from Chicago searching for a modern loft-like house, and we designed a vertical home with high ceilings to give them a taste of their former hometown. The dramatic steel and cable railings with wood top are very open, allowing energy to flow visually; instead of having a solid mass for stairs, these energetically float to anchor the space. Our clients also loved saffron colors and after presenting us with a petal picked off a sunflower, we began our search for coordinating pieces. The yellow Odegard rug and large painting add to the home's colorful depth.
Photographs by Peter Bastianelli-Kerze

Jane-Page Crump is president and lead designer of Jane Page Design Group. The award-winning, full-service interior design firm is well known for its elegant and distinctive work. For more than 25 years, the creativity and uncompromising standards of Jane Page Design Group have made the firm one of the most respected in the industry. To effectively serve its impressive client list, which includes many Fortune 500 executives, celebrities and political notables, the firm follows a team approach. The designers work closely with the finest contractors and architects to ensure that their clients' visions are met. Jane-Page Crump is a past president with the ASID Gulf Coast chapter, a past president of the Texas Association for Interior Design and has held numerous positions on both boards.

Jane-Page Crump est la présidente et principale décoratrice du groupe Jane Page Design Group. La société de décoration intérieure primée et à service complet est bien connue pour ses œuvres élégantes et distinctives. Depuis plus de 25 ans, la créativité et les normes intransigeantes de Jane Page Design Group ont fait de la société l'une des plus respectées du secteur. Pour servir efficacement son impressionnante liste de clients, dont de nombreux cadres de sociétés du groupe Fortune 500, des célébrités et des personnages politiques, l'entreprise adopte une approche reposant sur le travail d'équipe. Les décorateurs travaillent en étroite collaboration avec les meilleurs entrepreneurs et architectes pour veiller à respecter la vision de leurs clients. Jane-Page Crump a été présidente de la section de la Côte du Golfe de l'ASID, présidente de la Texas'Association for Interior Design (l'association texane de la décoration intérieure) et a exercé de nombreux mandats au sein des deux conseils d'administration.

Jane-Page Crump es la presidente y diseñadora principal de Jane Page Design Group. La compañía de diseño de interiores de servicio completo, ganadora de numerosos premios, es ampliamente reconocida por sus elegantes y distinguidas obras. Durante más de 25 años, la creatividad y los estándares sin concesiones de Jane Page Design Group la han convertido en una de las compañías más respetadas de la industria. Para servir efectivamente a su extraordinaria lista de clientes, entre los que se encuentran diversos ejecutivos de compañías de la lista Fortune 500, famosos y políticos notables, la compañía utiliza una estrategia de equipo. Los diseñadores trabajan en estrecha colaboración con los mejores contratistas y arquitectos para asegurarse de que se respetarán las visiones de los clientes. En el pasado, Jane-Page Crump se desempeñó como presidente de la delegación de la Costa del Golfo de la Asociación de Decoradores de Interiores de EEUU (ASID, por sus siglas en inglés), presidente de la Asociación de Diseño de Interiores de Texas y ocupó numerosos cargos en ambos consejos de administración.

Jane-Page Crump

TEXAS

Above: Combining the subtle color and interesting textures found in the fabrics and furnishings make an elegant yet inviting formal living room. The custom carved stone fireplace with an inset antique mirror is the focal point and helps create the symmetry for the seating areas.

Facing page: Designed as a comfortable and relaxing retreat, this gazebo/pavilion area becomes a sanctuary for the homeowner in both winter and summer. Included is a stone sink, grill, side burners, under-counter refrigerator, ice maker and storage for rolling carts; the ceiling has electric heaters and a fan. The flooring design of the summer kitchen ties together all of the exterior entertainment areas and relates to the interior home floor patterns.

Previous Page: For a Colorado great room, furnishings were placed with consideration for the outside and are conducive to friendly conversation. All decorative light fixtures, as well as the carved-glass and bronze-stair railing were custom designed by Jane Page Design Group for the scale and style of this space.
Photographs by Rob Muir

"Exquisite rooms emerge when architecture, fabrics, art and the space's psychology are harmoniously melded."

—Jane-Page Crump

Right: My client requested an elegant formal powder room that would coordinate with the other formal entertaining areas of the home. Lit from below by small xenon lamps is an etched-glass panel that separates the vanity and toilet areas. A crackle cabinet, black granite floor, crystal bowl and wood veneer wallcovering add to the exquisite design of the space.

Facing Page Top: In a master bathroom of Roman proportions, a coffee bar, exercise room and water closet are among the many amenities. Attention is drawn to the butt-glazed window, which frames the view of the custom designed stone water wall. In order to make the room feel warm and comfortable, we chose stained and glazed custom cabinet and finishes, tile designs and a textural wallcovering.

Facing Page Bottom: High-rise living never looked as good as this elegant, high-style formal area. With a projector concealed in the ceiling, the living room doubles as a media room. When the lights dim, the projector drops down and the 100-inch screen—also concealed—unfolds from the ceiling.

Previous Pages: Designed for a busy family of four who enjoy cooking and entertaining, the kitchen is a culinary delight. In the design of this incredible kitchen, we combined painted and stained cabinets with a stainless and carved-stone range hood, a leaded-glass window and crystal chandelier. The long wall features two large cabinets with carved bonnet tops that resemble armoires. In addition to the refrigerator and freezer, the wall includes two microwaves, an additional oven, an LCD monitor and a concealed baking area.
Photographs by Rob Muir

" As a designer, one of my goals is to exceed the expectations of my clients and to lead them through a new adventure, with new information, regarding all things that are needed to complete their home's interior."
—Jane-Page Crump

Renowned for graceful, contemporary residential and commercial interiors that mix modern classics with unexpected finds from all eras, GunkelmanFlesher works on projects from coast to coast. The noted Minneapolis-based interior design firm today known as GunkelmanFlesher has established a New York satellite office under partner Andrew Flesher. Tom launched his design career in 1963 in North Dakota, opening his namesake Minneapolis-based practice in 1976. The 2005 addition of Andrew Flesher as principal initiated the next stage of the firm's evolution and ensures a long future of continued success. Tom and Andrew share an appreciation for modernism and take a highly curatorial approach to creating the strictly edited, extremely eclectic but tightly tailored environments for which the firm is now widely known.

Réputée pour l'harmonie de ses intérieurs résidentiels et commerciaux contemporains associant les classiques modernes à des trouvailles inattendues issues de toutes les périodes, GunkelmanFlesher travaille sur des projets d'une côte à l'autre. Cette société de décoration intérieure renommée de Minneapolis que l'on connaît aujourd'hui sous le nom de GunkelmanFlesher a établi un bureau satellite à New York avec son partenaire Andrew Flesher. La carrière de Tom dans le domaine de la décoration a commencé en 1963 dans le Dakota du Nord. Il a ensuite fondé son entreprise de Minneapolis en 1976. L'arrivée d'Andrew Flesher en 2005 en qualité de directeur marque une nouvelle étape de l'évolution de la société qui lui garantit un avenir de réussite ininterrompue. Tom et Andrew ont en commun une appréciation du modernisme et une approche très conservatrice des environnements strictement aménagés, extrêmement éclectiques mais étroitement personnalisés qui font maintenant le grand renom de la société.

Reconocido por interiores residenciales y comerciales refinados y contemporáneos, que combinan clásicos modernos con hallazgos inesperados en todas las áreas, GunkelmanFlesher lleva a cabo proyectos de costa a costa. La famosa compañía de diseño de interiores con sede en Minneapolis conocida actualmente como GunkelmanFlesher ha establecido una oficina de representación en Nueva York a cargo de Andrew Flesher. Tom comenzó su carrera de diseño en 1963 en Dakota del Norte, fundando la compañía que lleva su nombre con sede en Minneapolis en 1976. El ingreso de Andrew Flesher como director en 2005 inició la siguiente etapa en la evolución de la compañía y le asegura un largo futuro y éxitos continuos. Tom y Andrew comparten su admiración por el modernismo y aplican un enfoque de curador de museo a la creación de los entornos estrictamente editados, extremadamente eclécticos y firmemente adaptados que hicieron famosa a la compañía.

GunkelmanFlesher

MINNESOTA ▪ NEW YORK

Above: The whole apartment is an array of styles from different periods, all tailored and cleanly arranged to showcase the wonderful antiques encompassing the client's collection; upholstery elements recede into the background while contemporary sculptural pieces grab attention.
Photograph by Susan Gilmore

Right: A European-style concept, the kitchen was designed as furniture lined against the wall, with built-in cabinetry designed to resemble a hutch; an aniline-dyed birch floor of a warm, espresso brown shade provides contrast against the shaded white cabinetry.
Photograph by Susan Gilmore

Facing Page: The den is a compromise between the husband and wife in which clean upholstery with subtle patterns presents the ideal backdrop to showcase their collection of art. The sofa's single down cushion presents less visual noise, less distraction for the art.
Photograph by Susan Gilmore

Previous Page: In the living room of a home in Napa, California, French doors and floor-to-ceiling glass enhance the essential indoor-outdoor relationship. To keep the home very light, open and airy, we incorporated off-white furnishings. An inviting chair is flanked by a custom-designed console to the left and leather-covered Holly Hunt stool to the right.
Photograph by Ken Gutmaker

Above: Originally built as a library, the office was treated as a gallery and the renovation opened up the lobby with light; the owner's extraordinary art collection is on display throughout the office.

Facing Page Top: We blended traditional with contemporary, covering a wing chair with a striking pony hide; a warm color palette of mostly white along with sand and camel colors is consistent throughout the apartment.

Facing Page Bottom: The juxtaposition of formal against casual, contemporary against traditional, is resplendent in the classic living room. The 1880s' French table is flanked by antique Italian chairs, the glass coffee table is by Jean-Michel Frank and the turn-of-the-century antler light fixture is from a lodge in upstate New York.

Photographs by Susan Gilmore

Top & Bottom: The owner's office represents a collection of classic art and furniture from all different time periods. We placed the glass wall as a sound divider between the conference room and the office while the silver Arco lamp provides the perfect amount of light. Two green Milo Baughman chairs and a sofa designed by Andrew Flesher afford ample seating around the glass coffee table.

Facing Page: Placing a little banquette area in the kitchen by the window created what has become a favorite spot to relax with guests. Albeit new, the banquette was given a mature look to be consistent with the classic architecture of the building.
Photographs by Susan Gilmore

" Significant design comes from passion for beautiful materials, attention to proportion, color and detail. An exceptional interior reflects the lifestyle of the client."

—Andrew Flesher

A big part of the business of interior design is developing relationships. This starts in the office. Jones-Keena & Co. is an eclectic group of designers known for interiors that sample every different style, that find unique personalities within each genre. The ability to zone in on the lifestyle of each client has allowed the team to create the highest quality projects with the highest business integrity. Never restricted to its home state of Michigan, Jones-Keena & Co. has, since 1991, guided homeowners on personal journeys of discovery. Founded by Lucy Earl, the firm produces individual projects through its lead designers, Nicole Withers, Ian Hartwell, Robert Endres—and Lucy herself. The bar for fabulous spaces has definitely been raised.

Le développement de relations est un aspect très important du secteur de la décoration intérieure qui commence au bureau. Jones-Keena & Co. est un groupe éclectique de décorateurs renommé pour ses intérieurs qui touchent à tous les styles différents et mettent en valeur des personnalités uniques dans chaque genre. La capacité à identifier précisément le style de vie de chaque client a permis à l'équipe de réaliser des projets de qualité supérieure avec l'intégrité commerciale la plus élevée. Jones-Keena & Co. ne s'est jamais confinée aux limites de son état d'origine, le Michigan, et guide les propriétaires sur la voie de la découverte personnelle depuis 1991. Fondée par Lucy Earl, la société conduit des projets individuels par l'intermédiaire de ses principaux décorateurs, Nicole Withers, Ian Hartwell, Robert Endres, et Lucy même. La barre des espaces fabuleux a sans aucun doute été relevée.

Una parte considerable del negocio de diseño de interiores consiste en el desarrollo de relaciones. Todo comienza en la oficina. Jones-Keena & Co. es un grupo ecléctico de diseñadores, conocidos por interiores que presentan elementos de cada estilo y encuentran personalidades diferentes dentro de cada género. La capacidad de concentrarse en el estilo de vida de cada cliente ha permitido al equipo crear proyectos de la más alta calidad con el mayor nivel de integridad de negocios. Jones-Keena & Co. no se circunscribió jamás a los límites de su casa matriz en el Estado de Michigan y desde 1991 viene guiando a propietarios en viajes personales de descubrimiento. Fundada por Lucy Earl, la compañía produce proyectos individuales a través de sus diseñadores principales, Nicole Withers, Ian Hartwell, Robert Endres y la misma Lucy. Definitivamente han elevado los estándares para la generación de espacios fabulosos.

Jones-Keena & Co.

MICHIGAN

Above: A young couple with small children wanted an inviting, warm family room that could also function for big, family events. The mood is set with a colorful Sultanabad rug with an Oushak design. Midnight blue Venetian plaster walls create a dramatic background for the classic Charles of London sofas and antique Chinese daybed cocktail table.
Photograph by Gene Meadows, courtesy of Nicole Withers

Facing & Previous Pages: Really strong architecture—the barrel-vaulted ceiling of the living room—embodies the English country house. In the home of a bold couturier, we strove for an edited and clean look, with a color scheme that could perhaps mimic high-end couture fabric: Playfulness meets serious architecture. The Heffernan painting is a brilliant modern piece placed to offset the orange sofas. In the kitchen, the timbered cathedral ceiling is painted chartreuse, a strange and wonderful pairing with the blue and white of the antique porcelain pieces. And, again, searching for how our elements would read architecturally was a high priority; for instance, the custom, tiled central hood could only work in this space.
Photographs by Beth Singer, courtesy of Lucy Earl

"Any great project has a strong design team behind it. Design, architecture, construction—all collaborate to build a fine house."

—Lucy Earl

Above Left & Right, Facing Page: Spaces can be glamorous and elegant and still approachable. A good, unique style is found in a Grosse Pointe home. The dining room features a pair of antique consoles and matching gilt mirrors. A dolphin-based, round dining room table has French gessoed chairs. But small scale needn't be any less elegant and sophisticated. The living room's neutral gray hues with a hint of yellow in the drapery visually expand the space. Meanwhile, a lovely Venetian mirror in the foyer sets the mood for what can be found in the adjacent living room and throughout the house.
Photographs by Beth Singer, courtesy of Ian Hartwell

"Good interiors should represent a world view."
—Lucy Earl

"A meaningful part of the creative process is listening . . . choose an art piece that speaks to you."

—Robert Endres

Top & Center: A loft in Detroit was completely redesigned in a downsize move. The open kitchen is a terrific hangout for guests and cooks. The living room, as well, embodies open space, as the volume shoots up two stories.
Photographs by Beth Singer, courtesy of Robert Endres

Bottom: Metals, mohair, art and interesting shapes all set on an Oushak rug create a sophisticated, warm, eclectic room. The custom, hand-forged iron cocktail table meets metallic Venetian plaster on the walls; during the day the walls have a soft gold to them, while at night, silver peeks out against the gold.
Photograph by Beth Singer, courtesy of Nicole Withers

Facing Page Top & Bottom: I knew we had to have a fabulous piece in the living room—the volume of the wall and the minimalist furniture demanded it. Bo Barlett did the painting, and it is a great capstone for the mid-century modern room. The extensive library sits opposite the living room and is a contrast to the other's volume, offering malleable public or private spaces.
Photographs by Beth Singer, courtesy of Robert Endres

Word gets around quickly, especially when your clients tell everyone they know about the latest design by Kara A. Karpenske of Kamarron Design, Inc. Known for her open communication, creativity and innate ability to transform a dull space into a luxurious retreat, Kara has distinguished herself throughout Minnesota and beyond. Whether given a blank canvas or a seemingly inflexible architectural layout, somehow every space is re-envisioned to reflect elegance and functionality using the latest color trends, textures and furniture. Kara's upscale and lavish interiors are meticulously attended to—no detail is ever overlooked. Kara creates timeless designs by yielding to a home's particular region and incorporating the clients' personality and her impeccable taste.

La nouvelle se propage rapidement, en particulier lorsque vos clients parlent à tous ceux qu'ils connaissent des dernières créations de Kara A. Karpenske de Kamarron Design. Réputée pour l'ouverture de sa communication, sa créativité et sa capacité innée à transformer un espace terne en une retraite luxueuse, Kara s'est distinguée dans tout le Minnesota et au-delà. Qu'elle dispose d'une toile blanche ou d'une configuration architecturelle apparemment inflexible, elle parvient d'une manière ou d'une autre à réaménager chaque espace de sorte à en faire un exemple d'élégance et de fonctionnalité, à l'aide des dernières tendances, textures et pièces d'ameublement. Les intérieurs luxueux et généreux de Kara sont méticuleusement conçus. Aucun détail n'est jamais laissé au hasard. Les créations de Kara sont intemporelles dans la mesure où elle prend en compte la région particulière dans laquelle se trouve la résidence et y incorpore la personnalité des clients à l'aide de son goût infaillible.

Las noticias vuelan, especialmente cuando sus clientes le cuentan a todo el mundo sobre los últimos diseños de Kara A. Karpenske de Kamarron Design. Conocida por su estilo de comunicación abierto, su creatividad y su habilidad innata para transformar un espacio aburrido en un entorno lujoso, Kara se ha distinguido en todo el Estado de Minnesota y más allá. Ya sea que trabaje con carta blanca o con un plano arquitectónico inflexible, de alguna manera cada espacio es rediseñado para reflejar elegancia y funcionalidad mediante el uso de las últimas tendencias de colores, texturas y muebles. Sus interiores elegantes y lujosos son meticulosamente considerados, no se deja de lado ningún detalle. Kara crea diseños atemporales al favorecer a una región particular del hogar e incorporar la personalidad del cliente y su gusto impecable.

Kara Karpenske

CALIFORNIA ■ NEVADA ■ MINNESOTA

Above: When I first approached the living room, I realized that its small scale required specific elements to give the illusion of more space. Clean lines and armless chairs contribute to the room's continuity, and a raised fire pit framed in black walnut works well with a colorful design scheme. Its vegetable-dyed rug, velvet window treatments and all new eight-piece trim add a timeless and refined ambience.

Facing Page Left & Right: We wanted the house to greet its guests with a rustic ambience mingled with modern accents. A slate floor, natural stone wall, barrel-vaulted ceiling and two arched lanterns offer a distinct expression in the space. A vine theme is carried throughout the space in the crystal chandelier and antique burnished silver tree leg table. A modern statuary-style table pairs well with fuchsia accent colors and a zebra rug.

Previous Page: When we first started renovating the old Minnesota farmhouse, we discovered that it was the first home built in what is today a very upscale part of the state. Taking this historicity into consideration, we wanted the interior spaces to reflect some of the original features. We kept the original hardwood floors and designed the medallion to give some added historical depth to the kitchen. Natural black walnut cabinets work well with countertops made of Carrera marble—materials seen in older homes—but we also added some modern features such as stainless steel appliances, honey onyx on the backsplash and a few statues. Contributing to the home's rich historical feel is an impressive light fixture hanging over the sink; originally, it had an oil-rubbed bronze finish, but it complements the space much better in its silver patina.
Photographs by Bill Diers Photography

"By blending natural materials and organic details, a distinct authenticity can be created in any space."

—Kara Karpenske

Above: An unintelligent use of space caused us to re-design the entire bathroom. Given that it was a small space, we relocated the shower and began creating a warm and accessible space. Custom tiles, a square backdrop behind the bathtub and the use of travertine, quartzite, glass inserts and bronze fixtures all contribute to the room's modernity and simultaneous elegance. A stone fish complements the fossilized plaque art, and leopard accent towels add a bit of kick.

Left: Space constraints led me to design a luxurious wet room for my clients' bathroom. Floor-to-ceiling glass walls contain humidity and offer a luxurious bathing experience reminiscent of a spa. To keep the space natural and simple, I incorporated his-and-hers vanities, travertine stone, basket-weave tile detailing and a few simple cherry blossom sticks. Overall, the room is more functional with re-arranged elements and a lighter color palette.

Facing Page Top: When a husband and wife have different stylistic preferences, it's an exhilarating challenge to create not just a happy medium but rather a design that functions and looks incredible. I blended the comfort of traditional furniture with the pizzazz of contemporary lamps and accessories; it's a custom blend that makes everyone feel at home. The striped silk drapery is carefully hung from five medallions to frame the picturesque natural surroundings.

Facing Page Bottom: A total remodeling effort went into a bathroom whose classic 1980s' décor was extremely outdated. Now the homeowners have a bright bathroom with natural stone, green granite, light colors, frosted and clear glass accents and framed mirrors with set-in sconces. The bathtub is definitely a focal point—it's undeniable that the clean and modern aesthetic is a stunning transformation.
Photographs by Bill Diers Photography

"Warm and inviting spaces evolve with a subtle application of classic sophistication, clean lines and generous proportions."

—Kara Karpenske

Top: My clients bought their home to preserve its history, and as part of its extensive renovations, we incorporated all new black granite and cherry cabinets, but chose to keep the natural floor. The multicolored backsplash complements the tile places above the cabinetry—this element makes the space feel larger and brings continuity to a thoroughly modern kitchen.

Center: When I first saw the metallic floral wallpaper, it reminded me of a home where everything harmoniously flows together. The design's gentle movement allowed the roof's intrusions to be softened and also elongated the space. A Zen ottoman, Asian console table and accent pillow all contribute to a guestroom that's inviting and relaxing.

Bottom: Rustic and natural, the kitchen's hickory floor and warm palette offers a bright yet cozy gathering place. The black walnut cabinetry with glass uppers is finished in a charcoal stain and elegantly accented by a copper and glass tile backsplash. Bringing a distinct definition to the classic and chic kitchen are its granite countertops, contemporary pendant lighting and top line appliances.

Facing Page Top & Bottom Left: The basement's low, seven-foot ceilings, one window and rectangular shape were a challenge. To maximize the area, I used small bracket panels and a soft blue-green color on the walls. Three-dimensional art on the wall serves as a great accent with the more traditional fabric on the cream mohair chair. Simple features—an Asian console, a natural fern, garden stools and simple pear accessories—transition to an adjoining bar whose modern brick-patterned glass make the area a great place for entertaining.

Facing Page Bottom Right: Just off the kitchen is a small kitchen eat-in area with extra wide doors that open out to a large deck and patio. Silk curtains and coral back armchairs complement the black table. We chose to anchor the stunning capiz shell chandelier with a ceiling medallion; off-setting the space is a zebra rug.
Photographs by Bill Diers Photography

Merging traditional, transitional and modern styles to create beautiful environments is what Cheryl Nestro does best. Her classic and timeless solutions are a direct result of her intuitive understanding of people's needs and their spaces' demands. Though Cheryl certainly has her own aesthetic preferences, she is conscientious to balance her professional opinions with homeowners' unique desires. She offices from her boutique studio and showroom, Tutto Interiors, where guests immediately catch a glimpse of the vision that's been stirring in her mind. All about using only the highest quality of furnishings, lighting, accessories and wall art, Cheryl is constantly on the lookout for new and extraordinary ways to depart from the ordinary. Unsurpassed comfort, quality and warmth echo within the walls of each project she designs.

La fusion des styles traditionnels, transitionnels et modernes est sans doute la spécialité de Cheryl Nestro. Ses solutions classiques et intemporelles sont l'aboutissement direct de son appréhension intuitive des besoins des personnes et des exigences de leurs espaces. Même si Cheryl a certainement ses préférences esthétiques, elle prend soin de concilier ses opinions professionnelles et les souhaits uniques de ses clients. Elle travaille à partir de son studio boutique et salon d'exposition, Tutto Interiors, où les visiteurs peuvent immédiatement avoir un aperçu de la vision qu'elle a concocté pour eux. Cheryl met un point d'honneur à n'utiliser que des meubles, éléments d'éclairage, accessoires et œuvres d'art mural de la meilleure qualité, et est constamment à la recherche de nouveaux moyens extraordinaires de sortir de l'ordinaire. Un confort, une qualité et une chaleur inégalés émanent de l'espace de chacune de ses créations.

La especialidad de Cheryl Nestro es la fusión de estilos tradicionales, transicionales y modernos para crear entornos maravillosos. Sus soluciones atemporales y clásicas son el resultado directo de su comprensión intuitiva de las necesidades de las personas y las demandas de sus espacios. A pesar de que Cheryl definitivamente posee sus propias preferencias estéticas, tiene especial cuidado de lograr un equilibrio entre sus opiniones profesionales y los exclusivos deseos de los propietarios. Cheryl trabaja desde su estudio boutique y sala de exposición, Tutto Interiors, en donde los visitantes pueden inmediatamente apreciar la visión que habita en su mente. Cheryl insiste en utilizar sólo la más alta calidad de mobiliario, luces, accesorios y arte mural y busca constantemente nuevas y extraordinarias maneras de escapar de lo común. Cada uno de sus proyectos exuda una comodidad, calidad y calidez inigualable.

Tutto Interiors

Above: An impressive 177-by-31-by-105 inches, the Habersham Trevi media center has a commanding presence. Everything in the room had to measure up to the scale and beauty of the large piece, so I chose all of the elements, from fabrics to finishes, very carefully.

Left: A Brazilian cherry wood floor sets the stage for the massive Habersham Belmont library system. I designed the fireplace's tile work and finish to complement the Habersham pieces. A timeless Schonbek chandelier perfectly adorns the room.

Facing Page Top: I took a somewhat awkward, dated space from the 1980s and brought it into today's style with a brand new color palette. The pleated window treatments were extended to the full height of the ceiling, and the panels on the outside create the illusion that both windows were equal in height.

Facing Page Bottom: To update the space, I covered the painted wood mantel with tecstone, replaced the forest green tiles with tumbled stone and of course specified all new furnishings.

Previous Page: My client's original vision for the formal entry involved a strong mirroring detail to float up the mahogany stairway, but I guided the space toward a more textural approach. We put lace inside the panel and placed a lustrous champagne mist stone on top, which perfectly complements the Turkish travertine floors. I customized the Schonbek chandelier to add color but not overpower it; a third of the shimmer comes from amber Swedish cut crystals.

Photographs by Don Kurek

Above Left: We chose the furnishings in the living room very carefully, starting with the Hickory Chair sofa. My client loved clean lines and didn't want anything fluffy or oversized in the room. From that point, the additional pieces followed suit; chairs and leather embossed commodes sit on either side of the fireplace.

Above Right: I persuaded my client to choose a slate floor in the conservatory, and because of that choice it is now her favorite room in the house. The wetbar is a focal point, and the opalescent mosaic tile beneath the cabinetry is just one of many thoughtful touches in the space.

Facing Page: The beautiful custom art niches are definitely focal points of the dining room. Each is accentuated with luster stone using a stencil relief, which adds a wonderful dimension. The soft amber color perfectly complements the gold tones of the travertine floor.
Photographs by Don Kurek

"I think the most successful spaces strike a delicate balance between old and new."

—Cheryl Nestro

"Recognizing the past's subtle—and often subconscious—influences is the first step toward great design."

—Cheryl Nestro

Top: The entire entry was inspired by the grand scale of the circa 1883 Louis XVI-style mirror—it is positioned across from the grand stairway and sets the tone for the color palette and the home's very traditional style. We came across the mirror well before we broke ground on the project, but knew it was a must-have because of its intrinsic beauty, elegant carving detail, and potential to make a really powerful statement. It was definitely love at first sight and works very well with the rest of the entry space.

Bottom: I found a beautiful blue antique stone tile thinking I would display it in my boutique, but it was quickly purchased by clients with a fondness for the color blue. The homeowners weren't sure where to install the tiles but as their home began to take on its own personality, we found that the stone would work best in a bathroom. We used the stone as the inspiration and focal point, and the rest of the tile choices were made to complement it.

Facing Page: The Baroque-style mirror was integral to the powder room's design. Because of its tremendous size, and the necessary height of the wainscoting, I opted to forgo the crown moulding. The mirror nestles in perfectly and the sandstone wall finish really accentuates it.
Photographs by Don Kurek

Personally creating resplendent interiors that reflect each client's unique aesthetic sensibilities, Tulsa-based Zoller Designs & Antiques has carved its niche in a talented industry filled with notable design professionals. Owner Debbie Zoller leads a small yet highly skilled staff that has created distinctive, engaging interiors throughout Oklahoma, from California to Maine. Many trips to Europe have unearthed an array of remarkable pieces, particularly French and Italian finds, which fill the firm's remarkable showroom. This eclectic mix of antiques and reproductions ranges widely in price and style, accommodating an array of budgets and stylistic affinities. Truly it is the diversity of clients and projects that delights this firm, as it yields continually engaging opportunities to create professional interiors intimately tailored to reflect its clientele.

Zoller Designs and Antiques, basée à Tulsa, crée des intérieurs resplendissants qui traduisent les sensibilités esthétiques uniques des clients, et a su s'aménager un créneau dans un secteur dans lequel les professionnels talentueux notables sont nombreux. Debbie Zoller, son propriétaire, dirige une équipe réduite mais très qualifiée qui crée des intérieurs distinctifs et attrayants de la Californie au Maine, en passant par l'Oklahoma. De nombreux voyages en Europe lui ont permis de découvrir un grand nombre de pièces remarquables, en particulier en France et en Italie, qui sont exposées dans les salons de la société. Ce mélange éclectique d'antiquités et de reproductions varie grandement en termes de prix et de styles, et est adapté à un grand nombre de budgets et d'affinités en matière de style. C'est véritablement la diversité des clients et des projets que recherche cette société, dans la mesure où elle offre continuellement des opportunités stimulantes de création d'intérieurs professionnels intimement personnalisés en fonction des besoins d'une clientèle variée.

Zoller Designs & Antiques, con sede en Tulsa, personalmente crea interiores resplandecientes que reflejan las exclusivas sensibilidades estéticas de cada cliente, y se ha ganado un lugar en una industria talentosa repleta de notables profesionales de diseño. Debbie Zoller, su propietaria, lidera un pequeño pero altamente calificado plantel que ha creado interiores distintivos y atractivos en todo el Estado de Oklahoma, de California a Maine. A través de múltiples viajes a Europa, la extraordinaria sala de exposición de la compañía se ha poblado de una variedad de notables obras, particularmente de Francia e Italia. Esta mezcla ecléctica de antigüedades y reproducciones varía enormemente en precio y estilo, para satisfacer una amplia gama de presupuestos y afinidades estilísticas. El principal encanto de la compañía lo constituye la diversidad de clientes y proyectos, ya que genera continuamente oportunidades para crear interiores profesionales íntimamente adaptados para reflejar los gustos de su clientela.

Debbie Zoller

OKLAHOMA

Above: We designed the bedroom for a teenage daughter, wanting to give it a more contemporary, youthful feel. The headboard stripe aligns perfectly with the handpainted running wall stripe; the black-and-white houndstooth pattern in the pillows has also been handpainted on an adjacent wall.

Facing Page Top: We used 100-year-old reclaimed wood to create the stately cabinets flanking the fireplace; the beautiful oil painting above the fireplace is a focal point in the room yet with a push of a button rolls up to reveal a television.

Facing Page Bottom: In order to make a fairly large room with tall ceilings a little cozier we placed an alluring canopy over the bed and created several intimate spaces within the room; the martini chairs fronting the fireplace swivel and are ideal for enjoying a warm fire along with a great book.

Previous Page: Working within a newly constructed home, we sought to give the family room a warm, traditional look with great character, which was achieved through the use of ceiling beams, rich and inviting fabrics and a grand fireplace. We designed the four-piece ottoman with an all-encompassing finish so that it's comfortably elegant as separate pieces or as a unified whole.
Photographs by Rick Stiller

"By maintaining a well-stocked and updated resource room we are able to provide the latest and most luxurious furnishings and fabrics, in a wide range of styles and price levels, for the most discerning client."

—Debbie Zoller

Above: The kitchen originally featured a stark white palette and in the remodel we applied warm fabrics and wall finishes to create an inviting ambience. While the room exudes a Country French aura, we used a mix of traditional and transitional pieces, such as the metal bar chairs strapped with leather, to create an exceptional aesthetic.

Facing Page Top: In yet another room with very tall ceilings we added all the elements above the mantel to give the wall, a major focal point in the room, scale and interest; a remote-controlled flat-screen television is concealed behind the painting. The expansive gilt mirror opens up the room and adds weight to another large wall. We created the small custom sofa, a replica of the larger sofa, for the family dog.

Facing Page Bottom: The combination wood and leather bed expresses a masculine tone yet the more feminine fabrics provide balance. A combination of pillow shams and neck rolls emanates cozy refinement; his side features a stunning walnut chest while hers includes a softer, red and gold glass chest.
Photographs by Rick Stiller

"Whether it is functional task lighting or purely decorative, lighting is an essential element of good design."

—Debbie Zoller

Top: The desire to emphasize the immaculate groin-vaulted ceilings led to the use of wonderful paint finishes and large light fixtures, the scale of which is ideal for the hallway. We broke up the corridor by the placement of a display cabinet, which is flanked by wing chairs, in addition to a small bench and a large Italian-themed painting.

Bottom: In a small man's study we created a well-proportioned, masculine feel through the walnut desk with rounded ends, the tall floor lamp and carved wooden warrior with black lamp shade. The carved, handpainted sculpture adds a splash of contemporary to the room's traditional aesthetic; the maple bookshelf adds weight to the wall yet the glass shelves exude a light, airy feel that emphasizes the eclectic accessories.

Facing Page: To make a fairly small room feel more open we barrel-rolled the ceiling, which is adorned with a trompe l'oeil, to which we applied plaster for a dimensional look. Formal but not stuffy, the room features red walls that lend great drama to the space; the finishes are done with a variety of paints and textures providing additional visual and tactile interest.

Photographs by Rick Stiller

In the early 1970s, Colorado was truly a virgin state for quality designers. Mickey Ackerman considers himself lucky to have landed in the midst of such a tabula rasa. More than 5,000 projects later, Amirob Architectural Interior Designers, Mickey's firm, finds itself still designing for the sake of the individual. All these years later, Mickey and his team design as though they never found their niche—so they do everything, from powder rooms to hotels, with a roster of notable executives and high-profile celebrities. There are great rewards in this diverse work, for as the market changes, so does Amirob.

Au début des années 1970, le Colorado était véritablement un état vierge de designer de qualité. Mickey Ackerman s'estime heureux d'y être arrivé alors que tout y restait encore à faire. Plus de 5000 projets plus tard, Amirob Architectural Interior Designers, le cabinet d'architecture de Mickey, sert encore des clients individuels. Après toutes ces années, Mickey et son équipe travaillent toujours comme s'ils n'avaient jamais trouvé leur créneau : ils font de tout, des cabinets de toilette aux hôtels, pour une longue liste de cadres de haut niveau et de célébrités. La diversité de ces travaux n'en est pas moins gratifiante, dans la mesure où Amirob change avec l'évolution du marché.

A comienzos de la década del 70, Colorado representaba un territorio verdaderamente virgen en cuanto a diseñadores de calidad. Mickey Ackerman se considera muy afortunado de haber tenido la oportunidad de haber hecho pie en dicha tabla rasa. Después de más de 5.000 proyectos, Amirob Architectural Interior Designers, la compañía de Mickey, continúa diseñando en beneficio del individuo. Después de todos estos años, Mickey y su equipo siguen diseñando como si nunca hubieran encontrado su nicho. Hacen de todo un poco, desde baños pequeños hasta hoteles, con una lista de clientes que incluye ejecutivos notables y famosos de gran exposición. Existen grandes recompensas en ese trabajo diverso, porque a medida que el mercado cambia también lo hace Amirob.

Mickey Ackerman

COLORADO ■ ARIZONA

"There is a bit of the collector in each of us."

—Mickey Ackerman

Above: To keep the kitchen as the soul of the home, we strove for a furniture look. The Italian sword wood, standing visible against black ceiling and wall, creates great conversation. Each piece of the room begs to be looked at independently.

Facing Page Top: A lack of exterior views, this Old World suite is a textural experience—the illusion of centuries is felt in the soffit, the blood-red walls and black glazing.

Facing Page Bottom: A visual experience: Trying to capture the exterior, the interior reflects some of the breath of the gorgeous mountains. Wall fabric adds a dramatic texture, while a cherry wood and cane bed gives an Asian flair.

Previous Page: Condo urban living does not have to be modern. Denver's contemporary museum plaza is the backdrop for an eclectic, warm interior. The view is an extension of the carefully placed arts—treasures collected from around the world.
Photographs by Eloy Minjarez

Top: Right off a working study, an intimate alcove is a great place to catch up on some reading. Liquid metal paint ages the room, giving it interesting character.

Bottom: Every guest experiences the powder room, and so we had a lot of fun creating a remarkable one. The pump-style sink faucet, serene wood elements and delicate handpainted mural reflect old European charm.

Facing Page Top: Tuscan influences are in vogue. The stone walls are real—the same as the outside materials—and, combined with an Italian bed, unique nightstands and hand-carved limestone fireplace, the room has a feeling of authenticity.

Facing Page Bottom: A lot of designers hide modern technology. However, social rooms should not look austere: The 120-inch screen seems at home with the hand-carved Spanish table. Indoors or out—Denver has eight months of patio weather—a home's spaces should be warm and inviting.
Photographs by Jim Blecha

"Interior design is the creation of illusion."

—Mickey Ackerman

Since 1998 Jorge Castillo has been designing his way around Cleveland and out of state. The trek to Ohio was long, however. A native of Mexico, Jorge attended college in Mazatlan, with the intention of studying architecture. But once he made his way through the interiors section of the program, he decided to stay indoors. His penchant for architecture, though, never left. Following family, he wound up in Ohio, where he enrolled into an interior design program and, finally, founded Jorge Castillo Design. With a majority of his work new construction, Jorge finds himself working with the shells of homes, and his blending of diverse interior design with remarkable architecture has become a veritable signature of his firm.

Depuis 1998, Jorge Castillo décore des résidences de Cleveland et à l'extérieur de l'état. Il a pris des chemins détournés pour arriver dans l'Ohio. Originaire du Mexique, Jorge a fait ses études à Mazatlan, en commençant par le domaine de l'architecture. Une fois familiarisé avec la partie du programme consacrée aux intérieurs, il a décidé d'en faire sa carrière. Son penchant pour l'architecture ne l'a toutefois jamais quitté. Il a suivi sa famille dans l'Ohio, où il s'est inscrit dans le cadre d'un programme de décoration intérieure, avant de fonder Jorge Castillo Design. Il travaille essentiellement sur de nouvelles constructions, à partir de la structure seule des résidences, et son association de créations intérieures diverses à une architecture remarquable est devenue la marque de sa société.

Desde 1998, Jorge Castillo ha practicado diseño en Cleveland y fuera del estado. Sin embargo, la travesía a Ohio fue prolongada. De origen mexicano, Jorge asistió a la universidad en Mazatlán con el objetivo de estudiar arquitectura. Pero una vez que pasó por la sección de interiores del programa de estudio decidió dedicarse de lleno a ellos. Sin embargo, su pasión por la arquitectura nunca lo abandonó. Siguiendo a su familia, terminó en Ohio, en donde se inscribió en un programa de diseño de interiores y finalmente fundó Jorge Castillo Design. Debido a que la mayor parte de su trabajo consiste de construcciones nuevas, Jorge debe trabajar con las cáscaras de los hogares; su amalgama de un diseño de interiores variado y una arquitectura extraordinaria se ha convertido en el estilo característico de su compañía.

Jorge Castillo OHIO

Above: Dreamlike, the dining room was inspired by the central painting. The room is almost colorless to highlight the blue of the painting, offset only by the red goblets. I designed the mirrors and the console, and tailored the chandelier to match the dreamlike effect. Mylark foil covers the wall, meeting the translucent wall treatment for an ethereal feel.

Facing Page: The home is tied together through its structural column element. Its grayish manifestation divides the kitchen, soaring back inward, while a light version separates the sleepers in the bedroom and a dark version outlines passages in the powder room. The kitchen was designed for contrasting tones, with a distinct sense of black and white. The bedroom was too long, so I portioned the room, leaving a corridor as a gallery space. The powder room is mirrored in 24-inch squares with beveled edges for an intense texture—and with the dark wood columns, the room carries over the great division of elements, much like the rest of the home.

Previous Page: The homeowners had a home on this property for 25 years, but they wanted their dream home here. So we took down the old and brought in the new. The owners already had the cantilevered side table and the coffee table, so I molded the home around that aesthetic. The table's angles are reflected in the staircase's architecture, while aquariums bookend the mantel. Even the take on the Rembrandt painting, *X-Rays Have Revealed . . .* by Ken Aptekar, is a modern interpretation of the traditional.
Photographs by Bill Webb, Infinity Studio

"Good interior design also incorporates the architectural details."

—Jorge Castillo

"Achieving design goals is about embracing the freedom you get from a homeowner."
—Jorge Castillo

Top & Bottom: Without the staircase, your eye would wander all around the narrow hallway and long foyer. But the circular nature of the stairs helps you focus on entry; then you can take your time and absorb the rest of the home. With views out to the lake and the river, the home's organic materials contrast with the off-white spaces. The mother-of-pearl tile shoots up two floors and nods to the natural world.

Facing Page: The homeowners wanted a sense of 1940s' California—that Old Hollywood glamour. The ground-up project was grand occasion to bring that golden era to Great Lakes region. The architecture allowed for great niches—perfect nooks for color against clean, modern furniture.
Photographs by Bill Webb, Infinity Studio

For the past decade Michael Del Piero has fulfilled her passion for interior design and refined her distinctive, engaging aesthetic. Under her guidance as principal, her firm, Michael Del Piero Good Design, was founded on the fundamental maxim that true client satisfaction is ultimately derived through a personal and highly communicative relationship between the designer and client—and an unwavering dedication to excellence in each project. She maintains that creating the right mood in a space is essential, be it a mood of serenity, a touch of romance or other. Her unique style and ability to interpret people's desires to create harmonious, sophisticated interiors have earned acclaim from discerning, high-end clients in New York, Chicago and Buenos Aires.

Michael Del Piero s'adonne depuis dix ans à sa passion pour la décoration intérieure et peaufine depuis son esthétique séduisante et distinctive. Sous sa direction, sa société, Michael Del Piero Good Design, a été fondée sur la base du principe selon lequel la véritable satisfaction du client provient en fin de compte d'une relation personnelle et extrêmement communicative entre le décorateur et son client, ainsi que d'un dévouement inébranlable en faveur de l'excellence dans le cadre de chaque projet. Pour Michael, il est essentiel d'insuffler une atmosphère appropriée dans un espace, qu'il s'agisse d'un sentiment de sérénité, d'un brin de romance ou d'autre chose. Son style unique et sa capacité à interpréter les désirs des gens pour créer des intérieurs harmonieux et sophistiqués lui ont valu les éloges de clients avisés et de haut niveau à New York, Chicago et Buenos Aires.

Durante la última década, Michael Del Piero ha trabajado para satisfacer su pasión por el diseño de interiores y refinar su particular y atractiva estética. Bajo su guía como directora, su compañía Michael Del Piero Good Design fue creada según el principio fundamental de que la verdadera satisfacción del cliente deriva de una relación personal y altamente comunicativa entre el diseñador y el cliente, y una constante dedicación a la excelencia en cada proyecto. Sostiene que la creación del ambiente adecuado en el espacio es esencial, ya sea un ambiente de serenidad, un toque de romance o cualquier otro. Su exclusivo estilo y su capacidad para interpretar los deseos del público para crear interiores harmoniosos y sofisticados le valieron la aprobación de exigentes clientes de alta gama en Nueva York, Chicago y Buenos Aires.

Michael Del Piero

ILLINOIS

Above: We set a modern Italian sofa and textured herringbone chairs around a two-tiered acrylic coffee table I found in Buenos Aires. I had the stunning armoire made from 17th-century doors from India.

Left: Antique Chinese and Korean pots and blown glass spheres adorn a circular table made of steel and reclaimed fir, which is surrounded by Gió Ponti chairs covered in slate blue mohair.

Facing Page Top: The residents' love of organic, modern and traditional furnishings is evidenced perfectly in the family room. The multilevel coffee table is comprised of wooden pedestals I found in Buenos Aires, which we laid on the floor in various formations and are played on by the children. The hand-forged iron chair was made by the Argentinean luminary Jose Thenee.

Facing Page Bottom: Oversized chairs woven from bent wood afford great interest and engender a natural aesthetic in the bedroom, which was inspired by the small table we found in New York. A plush bed is flanked by a pair of mid-century American nightstands with Lucite handles.

Previous Page: The dining room had an austere yet romantic mood, so I wanted to maintain and enhance that tone rather than change it. Perfect for family gatherings, the floor is comprised of vintage slabs of walnut while the Argentine table is made of old planks lacquered in graphite gray.
Photographs by Janet Mesic Mackie

Top: I combined Japanese, Korean and Chinese antique pottery for a wonderful earthen quality and their complementary colors.

Bottom: The residents had the bowl in their garden and I thought it would be great inside on the table. The tablecloth is a vintage Fortuny fabric we had made from old drapes; I had the glass spheres blown for the project.

Facing Page Top: When we were unpacking everything in the room, I placed an array of signed pieces and other finds on the mantel and we liked it so much we just kept everything there. The 11-foot sofa is covered in crushed Belgian linen and the large nude is from Paris.

Facing Page Bottom: The dining room exhibits the wonderful, early 18th-century tapestry with sterling silver and 18-karat gold threads; it was stitched by nuns in northern France. The homeowners brought back a fabulous cloth from Africa, and we mounted it on the wall with a twig I found outside. The antique Italian candlelit fixture is a compelling focal point.

Photographs by Janet Mesic Mackie

"With thorough attention to detail and meticulous scrutiny shown in the selection of materials and furnishings for each environment, a continuum must be established along which lifestyles, personalities and aesthetics may connect."

—Michael Del Piero

For more than 35 years Charles Faudree has designed compelling interiors throughout the United States and Europe. Located in charming Tulsa, Charles Faudree Antiques & Interiors also includes a resplendent retail store with a host of eclectic antiques and contemporary pieces. Much like Charles' interiors, the store includes both casual and formal, old and new. While Charles' personal stylistic affinity is for French Country, he designs in all styles and loves new approaches—of course, he feels every home needs a few antiques for their warmth, heritage and Old World charm. Always seeking new challenges, Charles is still driven to create extraordinary interiors in his signature style.

Depuis plus de 35 ans, Charles Faudree conçoit des espaces intérieurs incontournables dans l'ensemble des États-Unis et de l'Europe. Parmi les intérieurs de Charles Faudree Antiques and Interiors conçus dans ses bureaux de la charmante ville de Tulsa, on peut citer un magasin de détail resplendissant agrémenté d'un grand nombre de pièces antiques éclectiques et modernes. Tout comme les intérieurs de Charles, le magasin associe le naturel et le sophistiqué, l'ancien et le moderne. Même si la préférence personnelle de Charles en matière de style se porte sur le style campagnard français, ses créations sont de tous les genres et il adore les nouvelles approches. Il lui semble bien sûr que toutes les maisons doivent arborer quelques pièces antiques qui leur donnent leur chaleur, leur héritage et leur charme du Vieux Monde. Toujours à la recherche de nouveaux défis, Charles s'efforce sans cesse de créer des intérieurs extraordinaires dans son style distinctif.

Durante más de 35 años, Charles Faudree ha diseñado interiores convincentes en todo Estados Unidos y Europa. Con sede en Tulsa, Charles Faudree Antiques & Interiors también incluye una resplandeciente tienda minorista con una variedad de antigüedades eclécticas y piezas contemporáneas. Al igual que sus interiores, la tienda incluye tanto lo casual como lo formal, lo antiguo como lo nuevo. Mientras que su afinidad estilística personal se inclina hacia el estilo campestre francés, sus diseños abarcan todos los estilos y aprecia los enfoques novedosos. Pero, por supuesto, considera que todo hogar necesita algunas antigüedades para lograr calidez, tradición y un encanto del viejo mundo. Charles siempre está a la búsqueda de nuevos desafíos y aún siente la necesidad de crear interiores extraordinarios en su estilo característico.

Charles Faudree

Above: Reproduction chairs frame the antique stool in front of the fireplace, which features a gold-framed painting over the mantel that is part of the client's collection of cow art. A French Country buffet in the corner is topped by matching tole lamps illuminating four framed botanicals on the wall.

Facing Page Top: A comfortable, light-filled library is ideal for curling up with a good book. We added a limestone top to the antique coffee table, which is surrounded by a Rose Tarlow lounge chair, a Dennis & Leen sofa and a geometric-patterned chair with Clarence House fabric.

Facing Page Bottom: A plush bed with an elegant baldachin over the top is the centerpiece of the pink-themed bedroom we designed for a young girl. The custom-made armoire in the corner is one of a pair and includes a sheared fabric by S. Harris in the window; an antique French chair and new lamps with custom shades complete the room.

Previous Page: The loves of my life, Nicholas and Ruby, are resting comfortably, warmed by the fire in antique French wing chairs covered with Fortuny fabric. The mantel is antique and made from French limestone; my annual Christmas décor includes a wreath with violins and mandolins I've collected over the years.
Photographs by Rick Stiller

Top: The bouquet of orchids and elm branches is accented by a massive green leaf. A green French commode beyond rests in front of a painting by Joe Niermann; the box on the desk is made from horn.

Bottom: A contemporary painting of St. Tropez by Zoun Knokki provides a burst of blue and green over the Swedish sofa. The small, Napoleon III-style table is by Dennis & Leen, while the sculpture on the pedestal is from the client's personal collection.

Facing Page: Fresh flowers rest in a terracotta urn atop the walnut gate leg table in my library. I bought the antique painting of the little Scottish boy 25 years ago; a tole chandelier and custom-made sofa covered in Pierre Frey are cherished pieces.
Photographs by Rick Stiller

"Rules are only made to be broken, so if you love it you can find a place for it."

—Charles Faudree

Striking the perfect balance between what homeowners think they want and what will be timelessly beautiful and functionally life changing requires a comprehensive approach to interior design. Suzanne Lovell has mastered that approach. An interior designer who trained as an architect, Suzanne has an expansive palette of ideas and expertise, which allows her to simultaneously envision the broad strokes and the fine details of projects. Though each is as unique as its residents, designs to Suzanne's credit subtly exude her love of cultures around the globe through sophisticated art, furnishings and textiles. She further explores her passions through her partnership with master handweaver Sam Kasten, with whom she created Twill Textiles, designing luxurious fabrics that are mill-produced yet look and feel handwoven. Suzanne's more than two decades in the industry have allowed her to develop an impressive network of artisans and craftspeople.

L'équilibre parfait entre ce que les propriétaires pensent vouloir et la beauté intemporelle et la fonctionnalité susceptible de changer la vie de son utilisateur exige une approche holistique de la décoration intérieure. Suzanne Lovell maîtrise cette approche. Cette décoratrice initialement formée dans le domaine de l'architecture dispose d'une palette complète d'idées et d'expertises qui lui permet d'envisager simultanément les grandes lignes et les petits détails des projets. Même si chacun d'entre eux est aussi unique que ses occupants, son amour des cultures du monde ressort subtilement des créations de Suzanne, sous la forme d'œuvres d'art, de pièces d'ameublement et de textiles sophistiqués. Elle explore également ses passions dans le cadre de son partenariat avec Sam Kasten, maître tisseur, avec qui elle a créé Twill Textiles, et conçoit des tissus de luxe produits mécaniquement mais qui ont l'apparence et le toucher du tissage à la main. Plus de vingt ans dans la profession ont permis à Suzanne de former un réseau impressionnant d'artisans et d'ouvriers spécialisés.

Lograr un equilibrio perfecto entre lo que los propietarios creen que desean y lo que resultará hermoso y atemporal y provocará un cambio de vida funcional requiere un enfoque amplio sobre el diseño de interiores. Suzanne Lovell domina tal enfoque por completo. Suzanne es una diseñadora de interiores con formación como arquitecta que dispone de un amplio catálogo de ideas y de experiencia que le permite simultáneamente imaginar las pinceladas gruesas y los detalles finos de los proyectos. A pesar de que cada uno es exclusivo, sus diseños exudan sutilmente su pasión por las culturas de todo el mundo a través de arte, mobiliario y textiles sofisticados. Suzanne explora sus pasiones trabajando en conjunto con el experto tejedor artesanal Sam Kasten, con el que creó Twill Textiles, diseñando telas lujosas producidas en plantas textiles pero con el aspecto y la presentación de un trabajo artesanal. Sus más de dos décadas en la industria le han permitido desarrollar una notable red de artesanos.

Suzanne Lovell

Above Left: Bringing together new pieces and family heirlooms, travel keepsakes and decorative pieces that have been collected over the years is a wonderful opportunity, but it requires objectivity in editing and creativity in developing the space's composition. In the living room, etchings that once belonged to Frank Lloyd Wright adorn panels that open to reveal a flat-screen television. The multicolored lacquer table is a memento of Hong Kong; it is elegantly juxtaposed by a new acquisition chair upholstered in hand-tufted silk leopard velvet.

Above Right: East meets West with the bronze Indonesian sculpture atop the 18th-century Chinese writing table and the collection of vibrantly colored cup plates, part of a family collection that helped to start the Sandwich Glass Museum in Massachusetts.

Right: The painted wooden deer heads from Indonesia add a touch of whimsy to the otherwise contemporary Bulthaup kitchen.

Facing Page: The dining room connects the open kitchen and trellised terrace. I chose a narrow plank dining table to promote conversation. Once dessert has been savored, everyone can easily transition to the outdoor sanctuary. The soothing atmosphere is created through landscaping, casual seating nooks, vintage Chinese lanterns and the 19th-century Kuan Yin, a symbol of compassion.

Previous Page: South American artist Vik Muniz's *After Gerhard Richter* commands attention. Muniz's contemporary piece—and others, like the vessel by Paul Chaleff—is balanced by antiquities from Asia and Europe. Textures are paramount: The suede sofa, silk rug, wing chairs in handwoven Sam Kasten fabric and pillows covered in silk fragments from the Ottoman Empire are complementary.
Photographs by Tony Soluri

Right: The master suite exemplifies the marriage of architecture and interior design. The bed's canopy reads as an architectural trim. By bringing the canopy all the way up to the ceiling, the room's full height is accentuated. Likewise, the hand-dyed, woven silk draperies are hung from the apex of the walls, which are upholstered in the same luxurious fabric.

Facing Page Top: Located on historic North Astor Street in Chicago's Gold Coast, the uniquely U-shaped home needed a complete renovation—windows were added to not only take advantage of the sprawling Lincoln Park views but also to bring natural light into the heart of the home. The circular stairway's exquisite bronze and steel balusters were cast on-site. As a counterpoint to the crisp metal finish, the walls were covered with goatskin panels. The geometry of the panels, stripe of the walls and curve of the balustrade create movement, interest, depth and a delightfully tactile experience. The floor is equally exquisite: an antique rug from India sits atop the quarter-sawn wood floors with Art Deco-inspired metal inlay.

Facing Page Bottom: The spiral stairway connects the formal living room with the casual entertainment space on the third floor. Though both areas have a certain sophistication to them, the combinations of colors, fabrics and finishes produce different ambiences.
Photographs by Alan Shortall

"Interior designs weave together a wonderful tapestry of people's lives—their travels, passions and tastes—by juxtaposing cultures and styles, even centuries."
—Suzanne Lovell

chapter four

chapitre quatre

capítulo cuatro

West

Born and raised in Boston, Judy Fox attended the New York School of Interior Design and Harvard University before arriving in Arizona nearly four decades ago, but the Scottsdale-based interior designer was so taken with the eclectic surroundings and aesthetics of the Southwest that she never left. In the many years since then, her firm, Judy Fox Interiors, has been helping clients enhance their lives through the design of elegant spaces that integrate subtle yet rich layers of detail. Judy is inspired by the resplendent surroundings that are her desert home, particularly in the colors and textures that comprise its arid setting, which provide an ideal canvas for creating gracious indoor and outdoor spaces tailored to the uniqueness of the Southwest.

Judy Fox, qui est née et a grandi à Boston, a étudié à l'école d'architecture intérieure de New York (New York School of Interior Design) et à l'université d'Harvard avant de s'installer en Arizona il y a près de quarante ans. La décoratrice d'intérieur de Scottsdale fut tellement séduite par la variété de cet environnement et l'esthétique du Sud-Ouest qu'elle n'en est jamais repartie. Tout au long des nombreuses années qui ont suivi, sa société, Judy Fox Interiors, a contribué à l'amélioration de la qualité de la vie de ses clients en concevant des espaces élégants incorporant des couches à la fois subtiles et riches de détails. Judy est inspirée par l'environnement resplendissant de sa maison dans le désert, en particulier les couleurs et les textures de ce milieu aride, qui forment une toile idéale pour la création d'espaces intérieurs et extérieurs raffinés adaptés au caractère unique du Sud-Ouest.

Nacida y criada en Boston, Judy Fox asistió a la Escuela de Diseño de Interiores de Nueva York y a la Universidad de Harvard antes de llegar a Arizona hace casi cuatro décadas. A la diseñadora de interiores con sede en Scottsdale le gustaron tanto los alrededores eclécticos y la estética del Sudoeste de EEUU que nunca se fue. En todos los años que pasaron desde entonces, su compañía, Judy Fox Interiors, ha contribuido a mejorar la vida de sus clientes mediante el diseño de espacios elegantes que integran sutiles y ricas capas de detalle. Judy encuentra inspiración en los alrededores resplandecientes de su hogar en el desierto, particularmente en los colores y texturas que forman el terreno árido, los que brindan un lienzo ideal para crear afables espacios interiores y exteriores adaptados a la exclusividad del Sudoeste de EEUU.

Judy Fox

ARIZONA

Above: The plush silk drapes covering the window are so exquisite it would seem almost a crime to draw them back, but the views to outside suggest otherwise. Throughout the day the drapes, hung on large iron poles with iron rings, change in appearance as they pick up different values and orientations of light, creating a kaleidoscope of hue and texture. I wanted the light fixture to appear like one you might find in a wine cellar, and the wrought-iron composition with beeswax candles conveys a sense of antiquity.

Facing Page Top: Medium-toned wood from floor to soffit creates a softness in a kitchen of just the right size and proportions. The hood over the stove features a handcrafted traditional Italian design and the travertine backsplash is accented with metal dots. The cabinets along the top of the kitchen are lit from within and used to display a collection of painted pieces the client acquired in Italy.

Facing Page Bottom: In order to create a comfortable ambience for the family room, we took windows out to give it intimacy and limit glare. The vibrant vineyard painting is a striking focal point and hangs over a remarkable fireplace made of Santiago marble, which is no longer quarried. We ebonized the sandblasted coffee table to provide durability and contrast with the room's abundance of wood; the ebony is also reflected in the large candleholders.

Previous Page: The intimacy of the corner is ideally suited for sharing a game of chess, a long conversation or poring over a good book. An abundance of wood exudes a tone of warmth and welcome, which is supplemented by the rich silk in the chairs and the drapery as well as a pair of candles to create a genuinely cozy aura. The bookshelf exhibits a portion of the owners' well-stocked library including an array of collectibles. The antique table was brought back from one of their European expeditions.
Photographs by Karen Shell

Above: Comfort abounds in a living room designed for leisure. A sense of relaxed elegance is conveyed through the scale and roundness of the chairs, the thickness of the mantel and hand-carved corbels, the heavy edge on the inlaid burl coffee table and the softness of the leather and chenille furniture. All of the wood is distressed so that it is very textural yet durable for carefree family living, and the fireplace is flanked by a combination of leather-bound books, Indian art and collectibles from various trips.

Right: French doors open up the room to take advantage of the compelling mountain views. Designed to provide an informal space in which the owners can relax and share their day, the space includes two beautiful tapestry chenille chairs with silk pillows that beckon the owners to enjoy a moment of repose. Durable yet chic, the crocodile leather ottoman says take your shoes off and put your feet up, but the excellent mountain views and engaging patio beyond say come outside and enjoy the majestic desert aura at dusk.

Facing Page: Guests who walk through the home's front door are met by a wonderful radius wall, which provides an ideal setting for the engaging sculpture. The space is characterized by a pronounced contrast in texture: the roughness of the Indian blanket against the very smooth drywall; the slick face of the sculpture subject's skin juxtaposed with the roughness of the attire; the roundness in the art stand and the smooth, curved pots against the coarse textures of the dracaenas; and the timber pole and wood corbels fronting the flowing forms of drywall—the aspect of rough against smooth is ubiquitous and compelling.

Photographs by Karen Shell

"As you walk through a house
you should be constantly
surprised and delighted."

—Judy Fox

Top: Large-scale leather furniture affords leisurely relaxation in the entertainment center. Curvilinear drywall forms are contrasted by peeled ceiling timbers. Wood provides additional contrast against the drywall via the wood doors, which also serve the very functional purpose of concealing the television and components.

Bottom: Entrance through the patio takes one right to the front door—but the engaging exterior ambience should delay the progression. Charming old doors are flanked by a soothing fountain, and stone, tasteful landscaping and restorative Southwestern air create an exquisite outdoor space.

Facing Page: We had to make sure there was ample space for two chefs to work, so we designed the kitchen with abundant counter space, a large center island with a prep sink and a farm sink in the breakfast island to accommodate the owners' culinary ambitions. The drywall ledge where the kitchen ceiling meets the great room provides space for displaying various mementos and reflects the wall configuration across the room, which houses the entertainment center. The sofa is upholstered in comfortable, distressed leather, which provides a subtle backdrop for the more complex patterns of the throw pillows.
Photographs by Karen Shell

Mitchell Freedland Design is internationally known for its architectural approach to interiors, all the while keeping a sense of warmth, comfort and functionality. The firm is defined by its timeless, classic and tailored interiors. While Mitchell is best known for contemporary style, he works in many genres with a common bond of creating environments that induce a clear, cohesive statement. Mitchell's use of materials, from floor to ceiling, and choice of color schemes reinforce his design vision. Geography, architecture, culture and the environment are other elements taken into consideration while customizing each design. Creating individuality is all in the details. Whether the project is a multiunit residential building, hotel or private residence, Mitchell is driven to capture the client's personality and objectives.

Mitchell Freedland Design est connu dans le monde entier pour son approche architecturale des intérieurs, qui conserve un sens de la chaleur, du confort et de la fonctionnalité. La société est définie par le caractère intemporel, classique et personnalisé de ses intérieurs. Même si Mitchell est bien connu pour son style contemporain, il travaille dans de nombreux styles, tous caractérisés par la création d'environnements qui expriment une vision claire et cohésive. Son choix d'utilisation de matériaux du sol au plafond et de gammes de couleurs réaffirme sa vision de la décoration. La géographie, l'architecture, la culture et l'environnement sont d'autres éléments pris en considération lors de la personnalisation de chaque création. L'individualité provient essentiellement des détails. Qu'il s'agisse d'un immeuble de plusieurs résidences, d'un hôtel ou d'une résidence privée, Mitchell s'efforce d'appréhender la personnalité et les objectifs du client.

Mitchell Freedland Design es reconocido internacionalmente por su enfoque arquitectónico a los interiores, al mismo tiempo que mantiene una sensación de calidez, confort y funcionalidad. La compañía es definida por sus interiores atemporales, clásicos y adaptados. A pesar de que Mitchell es reconocido por su estilo contemporáneo, su trabajo abarca diversos géneros con el compromiso en común de crear entornos que brindan un mensaje claro y cohesivo. Su uso de materiales, desde el piso al cielorraso, y su elección de combinaciones de colores enfatizan su visión de diseño. La geografía, la arquitectura, la cultura y el medioambiente son otros de los elementos que toma en cuenta para la personalización de cada diseño. La creación de la individualidad está en los detalles. Independientemente de si el proyecto incluye un edificio de residencias múltiples, un hotel o una vivienda particular, Mitchell apunta siempre a capturar la personalidad y los objetivos del cliente.

Mitchell Freedland

VANCOUVER

Above: Furnishings and artwork were curated to complement the grand scale of the Vancouver mountainside residence. A soft natural color scheme infuses a warm presence, all the while letting the art and collectables breathe within the space.

Facing Page Top: When a home's surroundings are just as impressive as its interior, I capitalize on that feature. Open views and floor-to-ceiling windows reveal scenes that add strong character and beauty to the waterfront penthouse in Vancouver.

Facing Page Bottom: Hues from a neutral palette typically have a relaxing and welcoming effect. I employed neutral tones along with sensuous forms to create a memorably calming experience for a spa retreat in Honolulu.

Previous Page: Sightlines can make a huge impact when visitors first walk into a residence—what's visible gives an impression of the entire home. The Vancouver penthouse's clean lines and careful lighting direct the eye into nearby spaces, creating anticipation and excitement upon entrance.
Photographs by Ed White Photographics

"If you attempt to compete with nature, you
will never succeed. Always embrace nature."
—Mitchell Freedland

"Imposing an architectural order where there is none brings cohesiveness to interior environments."

—Mitchell Freedland

Above: Smart use of glass and metal opens the space, allowing multilevel views within the entryway. The stair work minimizes any distraction that may exist with more traditional carpentry to emphasize the art collection of eye-catching geometric patterns.

Facing Page Top: Organic elements like wood and stone keep modern designs from feeling cold or inaccessible. The beautiful space in Honolulu maintains a warmth that is often lost in contemporary settings.

Facing Page Bottom: The architecture creates a heightened sense of drama, which enhances the intimate vibe of the conversation areas.
Photographs by Ed White Photographics

Top: A unifying palette of alabaster white brings a harmonious balance to the Chicago residence. Antiques and contemporary pieces live well together.
Photograph by Ed White Photographics

Bottom: Located in Los Angeles, the penthouse is an eclectic composition of design genres, all of which hold their own within the dramatic double-height environment.
Photograph by Ed White Photographics

Facing Page Top: Vivid jolts of color create a memorable ambience. Furnishings are clean and linear, enhancing the rectilinear geometry of the space in Tokyo.
Photograph by Aaron MacKenzie-Moore

Facing Page Bottom: I created a strong architectural vocabulary to anchor the Vancouver penthouse's entry hall. The tall floral composition softens the layering of elements.
Photograph by Ed White Photographics

"The use of classics imposes a sense of timelessness."

—Mitchell Freedland

With more than 30 years as the principal of Ledingham Design Consultants and four decades of interior design experience, Robert Ledingham is known internationally for his design philosophies. This sincere dedication is reflected in rooms that not only function well, but also exude comfort and project homeowners' individual styles. Ever the champion of restraint and proportion, Robert leads his design team to create spaces of timeless elegance. Experience and excellence are driving forces behind every design—with an extensive in-house sample and reference library and unlimited access to local and international sources, nothing is out of reach for Ledingham Design Consultants.

Robert Ledingham est à la tête de Ledingham Design Consultants depuis plus de 30 ans et travaille depuis quarante ans dans le domaine de la déclaration intérieure. Robert Ledingham est réputé dans le monde entier pour sa philosophie de la décoration. Son dévouement sincère à cette cause n'est pas seulement visible dans des pièces qui non seulement fonctionnent bien, mais également qui sont confortables et traduisent les styles individuels des propriétaires. Robert, qui se fait toujours le champion de la retenue et de la proportion, conduit des équipes de décorateurs qui créent des espaces d'élégance intemporelles. L'expérience et l'excellence sont les forces motrices derrière chaque création, ainsi qu'une bibliothèque interne complète d'échantillons et de référence, et un accès illimité aux sources locales et internationales, de sorte que rien n'est hors de la portée de Ledingham Design Consultants.

Con más de 30 años desempeñando el cargo de director de Ledingham Design Consultants y cuatro décadas de experiencia anterior en diseño, Robert Ledingham es reconocido internacionalmente por sus filosofías de diseño. Esta dedicación sincera se refleja en las habitaciones que no sólo funcionan adecuadamente sino también exudan confort y proyectan los estilos individuales de los propietarios. Robert es un eterno partidario de la moderación y la proporción y lidera a su equipo para crear espacios de elegancia atemporal. La experiencia y la excelencia son las fuerzas promotoras de cada diseño, con una amplia muestra, una biblioteca de referencia interna y acceso ilimitado a proveedores locales e internacionales; nada es imposible para Ledingham Design Consultants.

Ledingham Design Consultants

VANCOUVER

Above Left: The entrance rotunda to the master bath features wood paneling with curved sliding doors leading to the his-and-hers closets.

Above Right: The steam shower of the master bathroom features rich brown glass mosaic tiles contrasting with the beige limestone floors, a frosted glass panel over the exterior curtain wall provides plenty of natural light.

Facing Page Top: The penthouse's living room is a double-height space of glass capturing the panoramic views. Limestone floors, custom wool and silk carpet, silk, chenille and leather upholstery are combined in a subdued and textured color palette.

Facing Page Bottom: Extensive wood paneling is woven throughout the core of the apartment and carried into the family room. The television is built-in with speakers hidden behind a fabric panel. A chenille sofa, leather lounge chair and Christian Liaigre coffee table are oriented around the fireplace and its custom marble surround.

Previous Page: The dramatic penthouse suite's dining room captures the mountain and water views. Custom lighting was installed in the stepped skylight over the mahogany table and J. Robert Scott arm chairs.
Photographs by Ivan Hunter

"Whenever Mother Nature provides a stunning palette, an interior should always lean toward neutral tones."

—Robert Ledingham

Above: To add privacy but not obstruct any of the light, a sheer drapery was hung across the glass curtainwall. Two hanging mirrors are placed over the Flaminia porcelain sinks. The makeup area at the end of the vanity is well situated to utilize natural light.
Photograph by Ivan Hunter

Left: The lounge area in the master bedroom features a wood ceiling framing the view. Once again, textures of silk chenille and leather are showcased in subtle colors. A goatskin waterfall coffee table completes the space.
Photograph by Ivan Hunter

Facing Page: A False Creek renovation, the dining room features a restored 1930s' dining table; J. Robert Scott chairs add an Art Deco flavor to the space. The chandelier is period Murano glass and contrasted by the Warhol prints of Marilyn Monroe from the homeowners' collection.
Photograph by Ed White Photographics

Top: The elegant master bedroom includes a custom leather headboard and Italian bedding. Wood nightstands with custom hardware accent the Robert Kuo lamp.
Photograph by Ivan Hunter

Bottom: Shutters were placed on a window overlooking the city for privacy and for textural quality. Light emperador marble floor and dark brown emperador marble on the vanity make the space a desirable retreat.
Photograph by Ed White Photographics

Facing Page Top: The apartment's living room captures landscape views via a neutral palette—wool mohair sofas, custom glass coffee table and leather chairs. The buffet behind the sofa was custom made in Macassar ebony with shagreen doors. By using the Asian influenced Robert Kuo lamps, the room has simple, contemporary style.
Photograph by Ed White Photographics

Facing Page Bottom Left: The banquette, with a table and side chairs, makes a comfortable breakfast area. A large Italian Surrealist painting graces the wall.
Photograph by Ed White Photographics

Facing Page Bottom Right: The apartment foyer incorporates a dark brown emperador marble floor and wall paneling in Makore. The powder room door is built into the paneling to avoid any unsightly interruption to the space's ambience. Custom metal rods affix into the paneling reveals to hang the artwork.
Photograph by Ed White Photographics

Carol D. Williamson, founder of Carol Williamson + Associates Limited, practices a strong team approach to design both within her studio and with each of her clients. Avoiding project type specialization, she pursues corporate and residential projects for the gained experience within both disciplines. Her final design solutions evolve out of the desire to integrate her understanding of her client's individual environmental needs and her extensive design experience. Success follows with the careful play of architecture, light and complex, sophisticated color. Texture and pattern in the finishes and furnishings and the integration of each client's individuality complete CW+A's finished projects. When enthusiasm and creativity meet, it is a reflection of Carol's desire to create beautiful design solutions no matter what design style her clients request.

Carol D. Williamson, fondatrice de Carol Williamson + Associates Limited, met en œuvre une solide approche reposant sur le travail d'équipe, dans son studio de décoration comme avec chacun de ses clients. Elle évite de se spécialiser dans un type particulier de projet, et leur préfère des projets résidentiels et d'entreprise de sorte à acquérir une expérience dans ces deux disciplines. Ses solutions de décoration finies proviennent d'un désir d'intégration de sa compréhension des besoins individuels de ses clients et de sa vaste expérience de la décoration. La réussite découle du jeu réfléchi de l'architecture, de la lumière et de couleurs complexes et sophistiquées. La texture et les motifs des finitions et de l'ameublement, et la prise en compte de l'individualité de chaque client caractérisent les projets finis de CW+A. La rencontre de l'enthousiasme et de la créativité témoigne du désir de Carol de créer des solutions de décoration quels que soient les styles demandés par ses clients.

Carol D. Williamson, la fundadora de Carol Williamson + Associates Limited, practica un sólido enfoque de equipo para el diseño, tanto dentro de su estudio como con cada uno de sus clientes. Evitando todo tipo de especialización, se dedica a proyectos corporativos y residenciales para adquirir experiencia dentro de ambas disciplinas. Sus soluciones finales de diseño evolucionan a partir del deseo de integrar su comprensión de las necesidades ambientales individuales de sus clientes y su amplia experiencia en el área. El éxito surge a partir de la cuidadosa interacción de arquitectura, luz y color complejo y sofisticado. La textura y los patrones en las terminaciones y el mobiliario y la integración de la individualidad de cada cliente da el toque final a los proyectos de CW+A. Cuando se produce la conjunción de entusiasmo y creatividad, es un reflejo del deseo de Carol de crear bellas soluciones de diseño independientemente del tipo de estilo de diseño que soliciten sus clientes.

Carol Williamson

Above: The design for the master bedroom was developed when Carol's client requested a round bed to complement the curvilinear exterior glass wall. The custom iron and wenge bed was designed by Gregory Miller. Dark chocolate brown leather cushions surround the bed to provide additional seating. Soft white sheer drapes were hung at the windows as well as at the bed to create a room within a room for a more romantic efect.

Right: The penthouse's two-story living room provides an elegant but inviting place for the owner to relax and enjoy the exquisite views over the ocean. The deep blue and camel Gabbeh area rug set the tone for the palette of this room. Pale ivory leather with a rich textural blue and camel-patterned upholstery on the modern sofa complement the rich dark-framed wood lounge chairs and daybed at the windows' edge.

Facing Page Top & Bottom: The dining room on the main level of the three-story residence and the bar on the top level are set off by the warmth of the pale neutral limestone floors. Dark java stained furniture in both spaces provides a dramatic contrast to the mahogany paneling throughout. The use of onyx at the kitchen bar and tightly woven rattan on the dining chairs creates a rich contrast in textures and materials.

Previous Page: The elegant retreat is located on the top floor of a penthouse. The combination of pale limestone and warm mahogany paneling provides a rich backdrop for the collection of antique Japanese swords and artifacts. Neutral textured fabrics and pale aquamarine silk accents complement the dramatic ocean view.

Photographs by Stephen Cridland

Above: Located in Northwest wine country, the vineyard home was designed to be both rustic and elegant. Natural mahogany floors create a backdrop for the rough hewn wood beams and hemlock ceiling in the living/dining room. Custom wool area rugs and refined traditional furniture create a warm and inviting ambience.

Right: Located on the top floor of the residence, the master bedroom palette features saturated French blue and cream linens that complement the warm wood tones of the structural elements. The balcony features a panoramic view of the vineyards surrounding the residence.

Facing Page Top: Rustic cabinets with hand-hewn iron knobs are set off by vintage reclaimed terracotta floor tiles from France in the kitchen. Rich stone tops and handmade tiles from Pratt and Larson complement the texture of the natural stone wall. Natural fir windows frame the view of the vineyard.

Facing Page Bottom Left & Right: Custom iron and wood doors welcome visitors to the main level of the house. The wine cellar features a barrel-vaulted brick ceiling, with a tasting table with a deep terracotta-colored marble top. Iron pendant lights highlight the extensive wine collection displayed on custom wood racks.
Photographs by Stephen Cridland

"It is important that with every design, a sense of warmth, elegance and timelessness is created for each of our clients."

—Carol Williamson

Top: The owners of the Christensen 157-foot motor yacht requested an elegant contemporary interior design solution. Custom furniture was selected with modern lines that were influenced by traditional forms and accented with warm textural fabrics. Pale cream wool carpet was selected to contrast with the dark cherry wood paneling. The salon on the main deck of the boat is surrounded by panoramic windows that provide stunning views over the water.

Center: The dining room is open to the salon and features an impressive high gloss table that accommodates 12 guests. A soft, elegant persimmon color is featured in the subtle floral patterned silk on the dining chairs. A hand-applied, platinum-colored silver leaf ceiling feature accentuates this formal dining room.

Bottom: On the upper level of the boat, the sky lounge offers a more casual living space. The bar is complemented by the custom cream leather chairs and dramatic marble top, and allows additional dining by virtue of its custom height. A comfortable modular sofa and lounge chair provide an inviting place to look out over the water or watch television.

Facing Page: The seating area in the VIP stateroom on the lower level of the yacht is surrounded by cream silk wall panels and beautifully detailed raised-panel cherry woodwork. An elegant lounge chair and table provide a quiet retreat for guests. The silver leaf modern mirror captures the light from the porthole on the opposite wall of the stateroom.

Photographs by Stephen Cridland

After collaborating with architects and developers to produce innovative and functional designs for more than a decade, Tirzah Woods continues to place her hand in a variety of projects. Nothing is off limits for the principal of Woods Design Studio, whose portfolio boasts convention centers, medical offices, corporate headquarters, homes and more. She specializes in space planning, ergonomics, furniture and lighting and creates the optimum working and living environment for every client. At the end of each project, Tirzah bases success on the achieved ambience or efficiency within the space, as well as her clients' enjoyment and quality of life.

Après avoir collaboré avec des architectes et des concepteurs à la création d'intérieurs innovants et fonctionnels pendant plus de dix ans, Tirzah Woods continue à marquer de son empreinte une multitude de projets différents. Rien n'est hors de la portée de la directrice de Woods Design Studio, dont le portfolio comprend des palais des congrès, des cabinets médicaux, des sièges d'entreprise, des résidences et bien d'autres projets. Elle travaille plus particulièrement dans le domaine de la planification de l'espace, de l'ergonomie, de l'ameublement et de l'éclairage, et crée l'environnement de travail et de séjour optimal pour chaque client. À la fin de chaque projet, Tirzah mesure sa réussite à l'ambiance créée ou à la fonctionnalité de l'espace, ainsi qu'au confort et à la qualité de la vie de ses clients.

Después de colaborar con arquitectos y desarrolladores para producir diseños innovadores y funcionales durante más de una década, Tirzah Woods continúa participando en diversos proyectos. Nada está vedado para la directora de Woods Design Studio, cuya cartera de clientes incluye centros de convenciones, consultorios médicos, casas matrices corporativas, hogares y mucho más. Se especializa en planificación del espacio, ergonomía, mobiliario e iluminación y crea el entorno de trabajo y vivienda óptimo para cada cliente. Al final de cada proyecto, Tirzah evalúa el éxito en base al ambiente o eficiencia logrado dentro del espacio y al disfrute y calidad de vida de sus clientes.

Tirzah Woods

WASHINGTON

Above: Coming in the front entry and up the stairs, the clients wanted to have a gallery for their paintings and sculptures. We decided to keep the space very clean and minimal so as not to detract from the large canvases. Lighting the gallery was a challenge because it faces a street-side view and the clients didn't want to feel like they were living in a fish bowl at night; we used minimal lighting and balanced the large amount of glazing with a neutral palette that made the gallery feel warm and inviting.

Facing Page Top: We wanted the house to feel open, so we took the same approach with the master bedroom. The shoji screens are available for privacy as needed. Since most of the spaces blend into one another we continued the warm color palette but painted the wall behind the headboard darker to accent the roof line and give the room a sense of drama. Our overriding concern was to make sure the space yielded to the client's artwork.

Facing Page Bottom: One of the main design elements of the house was its four structural concrete walls. Originally they were intended to be left as unfinished concrete, but we decided to acid stain all sides of the walls, inside and out, and it's now one of the client's most beloved features. A seamless piece of curved glass encloses the shower, and a custom stainless steel Japanese soaking tub overlooks Chuckanut Bay; the circular hand-buffed finish on the soaking tub reduces fingerprints and water drops.

Previous Page: Wrapping between the living room and kitchen, the stone fireplace is a central focal point. To seamlessly incorporate the three-sided fireplace into the stone wall, we surrounded the fireplace with black granite and extended the mantel into the stone, melding the elements. The Buddha head set atop the fireplace is one the owner's favorite pieces.
Photographs by Rodrigo del Pozo

Above: The furnishings throughout the home are extremely minimal and durable: no decorative side tables or gratuitous accessories. Given the owner's love for color, patterns and unconventional materials, we paired the bold, red corrugated metal siding with a commercial carpeting that had vibrant colors and patterns. In the end, we tied all of the elements together with the porcelain tile floors, which were chosen throughout much of the house because they don't show paw prints or dog hair as readily.

Right: The main stairway connects the front entry to the second-floor living space and continues up to the master bedroom suite, so we needed to make the a dynamic space as it sets the tone for the rest of the house. To complement the copper entry flooring, we painted the light fixtures orange, and blue was added to the ceiling as a reflection of the quiet lake that the home sits on.

Facing Page: Having many relatives and two large rottweilers, the owners wanted a home that was dynamic, honest, uncluttered and durable. So part of the challenge was finding materials that would work with the design scheme but could also survive a love-filled beating from all their guests and either dog. Given the design criteria, most products throughout the home are commercial grade—from the carpet, linoleum and cable rails to the metal siding and copper vinyl tiles within the entry hall.
Photographs by Rodrigo del Pozo

"When a house has an abundance of wood, metal and glass, I often prefer to soften and quiet bedrooms with a natural-feeling carpet."

—Tirzah Woods

Top: My clients preferred built-in furniture for their master suite, so we designed a piece to make it architecturally interesting. Every aspect of the room is connected to the headboard so the owners can engage the fireplace, lights and blackout blinds without ever stepping foot on the floor. All of the bedroom materials and elements were simple and low maintenance: The porcelain tile surrounding the fireplace acts as a quiet counterpoint to the bed and patterned carpet.

Bottom & Facing Page: A softer shade of white was introduced in the master bathroom since it complemented the materials within the space better than the crisp white walls that were used throughout most of the house. Porcelain tile counters and the river rock backsplash are echoed in the steam room shower; the freestanding vessel tub looks out toward the lake. One of the bathroom's special features is the illusion of two large-scale windows thanks to a large mirror on an adjacent wall. Also, the linearity of the porcelain floor tile adds a unique texture to the space.
Photographs by Rodrigo del Pozo

Christine Archer was born to design. By living and breathing design, Christine embodies a personal philosophy that essential living requires an atmosphere that reflects the owner and is comfortable—the persona that is the beating heart behind a grand home. With a decade at the helm of Christine Archer Interiors, Christine encompasses what is great about the Pacific Northwest with each of her homes. Bringing the outdoors in, Christine utilizes wide expanses of windows to ensure that on those rainy northwestern days, nature still blankets our lives. This passion for our livable spaces translates to unique, eclectic homes in a remarkably fecund region of the country.

Christine Archer est une décoratrice née. Elle vit pour la décoration. Christine incarne une philosophie personnelle selon laquelle une vie essentielle exige une atmosphère confortable qui correspond au propriétaire, la personne derrière toute grande résidence. À la tête de Christine Archer Interiors depuis dix ans, Christine rassemble tout ce qu'il y a de positif dans la région Pacifique Nord-Ouest dans chacune de ses résidences. Elle concilie intérieur et extérieur grâce à de larges étendues de fenêtres de sorte à ce que lors de ces journées pluvieuses du Nord-Ouest, la nature reste présente dans nos vies. Cette passion pour nos espaces de vie se traduit sous la forme de maisons uniques et éclectiques dans une région remarquablement féconde du pays.

Christine Archer nació para el diseño. Christine vive y respira el diseño y hace suya la filosofía personal que sostiene que la existencia esencial requiere de una atmosfera que refleje al propietario, la persona que representa el corazón detrás de cada gran hogar, y que resulte confortable. Con una década al timón de Christine Archer Interiors, Christine representa lo mejor de la región del Noroeste del Pacífico con cada uno de sus hogares. Christine incorpora el aire libre a los interiores y utiliza grandes extensiones de ventanas para asegurarse de que en aquellos días lluviosos del Noroeste, la naturaleza siga impregnando nuestras vidas. Esa pasión por los espacios habitables se traduce en hogares exclusivos y eclécticos en una región extraordinariamente fecunda del país.

Christine Archer

WASHINGTON

Above: An open dining and living room aids the evening's flow from dinner to drinks. Some of the windows were lower, so carefully placed paintings maintain the sightline. A circular metal fixture gives a great accent to the light fabric drapes.

Right: To create a loft-like ambience, I dropped the abstract painting to the floor. Floors are a terrific way to put a surprise element in a home; the oak is stained with an espresso finish.

Facing Page: The dining room exudes intimacy. The chandelier and metal art piece have a great reflective nature to them.

Previous Page: I'm very traditional with a modern twist—current but classic—and the living room captures that. Homeowners want longevity through traditional large pieces, but achieve a current feel with the smaller pieces. The large mirror is a perfect capture of the greenbelt outside.
Photographs by David Duncan Livingston

Top: The home was all about contrasts. Deep, dark woods and fabrics interplay with subdued walls, objets d'art and sparkling finishing touches.

Bottom: The intention of the hallway was to reflect a lot of the natural light, contrasting with the walls. The sun-shaped mirror and the mirrored chest brighten the space.

Facing Page: Because of the high volume of the room, the ceiling is brought down with a chocolate brown. The huge crystal chandelier works like a beacon at night through the tall windows. So many people are rained in here that vast planes of windows bring mountains, trees and water in.

Photographs by David Duncan Livingston

"Everybody should love their home."

—Christine Archer

A quick look at the work of Timothy Corrigan makes it clear why he has been hailed in the press as "Today's Style-Setter." His fresh approach to design achieves a look that is both comfortable and elegant at the same time. By choosing never to compromise a space's livability for its aesthetic premise, he has reshaped his clients' surroundings to create individual worlds that reflect the way people want to live today. He synthesizes homes so that they not only celebrate their architectural nuances, but also provide a taste of numerous furniture and style periods. His philosophy is firmly grounded in eco-luxury, where environmental consciousness never sacrifices style, quality or effectiveness. A Timothy Corrigan home is not merely beautiful, but the entire entity is fully lived-in and enjoyed.

Un rapide coup d'œil sur le travail de Timothy Corrigan explique clairement les raisons pour lesquelles il a été salué par la presse comme le « créateur des tendances du jour ». Son approche innovante du design lui permet d'aménager des espaces à la fois confortables et élégants. En choisissant de ne jamais compromettre l'habitabilité de l'espace en faveur de considérations esthétiques, il réinvente l'environnement de ses clients pour créer des mondes individuels représentatifs du style de vie que ceux-ci souhaitent aujourd'hui. Il synthétise des maisons de telle sorte qu'elles ne se contentent pas de célébrer leurs nuances architecturales, mais qu'elles évoquent également différentes périodes de styles à l'aide de différents types de meubles. Sa philosophie est fermement ancrée dans l'éco-luxe, dans lequel la conscience écologique ne sacrifie jamais l'élégance, la qualité ou l'efficacité. Une maison de Timothy Corrigan n'est pas seulement magnifique, on y vit et l'apprécie pleinement.

Una mirada rápida al trabajo de Timothy Corrigan deja en claro por qué ha sido considerado en los medios como el "fijador de estilos de la actualidad". Su novedoso enfoque del diseño logra un estilo que resulta confortable y elegante a la vez. Mediante su decisión de nunca sacrificar la habitabilidad de un espacio en beneficio de su premisa estética, ha recreado los entornos de sus clientes para crear mundos individuales que reflejan la manera en que las personas viven en la actualidad. Sintetiza hogares de manera de que no sólo se destaquen sus matices arquitectónicos sino que también brinden una muestra de los numerosos periodos de mobiliario y estilos. Su filosofía está firmemente basada en el lujo ecológico, en el que la conciencia medioambiental nunca sacrifica estilo, calidad o efectividad. Un hogar de Timothy Corrigan no sólo es bello sino que la entidad entera es completamente habitable y digna de ser disfrutada.

Timothy Corrigan

CALIFORNIA

Above: The Georgia home's original color scheme had paneling and detailing of separate colors, but this caused the owner's extensive Sam Francis art collection to compete for attention with the walls. Interestingly, many Georgian homes, regardless of all architectural detailing, were actually painted one consistent color. With this knowledge, all of the walls were painted a bright, but plain, blue and an Irish Georgian console table and antique jars from Italy and Holland were added to provide an unexpected counter-balance to all of the contemporary art.

Facing Page: Inspired by its residents, leaders in the fashion world, the dining room is a continuation of the rest of the house and its seeping bright, bold colors. Starting with the traditional, clean lines of a set of Italian 18th-century Neoclassical chairs, each was upholstered in hot pink, electric blue, hot purple or green velvet. Because the space was very long, thin and not conducive to art pieces, high drama is delivered in the tented ceiling and upholstered walls with handpainted fabrics. Again, to pair the old with the new and add a bit of magic to the space, a custom-designed mirrored table and 1930s' chandelier finish off the room.

Previous Page: The Moorish architecture in the living room of Humphrey Bogart's former residence would have typically called for traditional, heavy furnishings of brown and gold tones, but we chose to work against those elements. Since the room was extremely dark—and as a Hollywood Landmark building, no windows could be added—I brightened the space through light colored upholstered furniture. A limed oak French coffee table from the 1930s paired with 18th-century French mirrors on the walls contribute to a stunning combination of periods. Another challenge was the room's 28-foot ceilings, and in order to complement the room's proportions, we designed a set of four-foot contemporary lamps. The resulting room is one that feels fresh, eclectic, and most importantly, very much alive
Photographs by Michael McCreary

Top: Designed for the creator of *Everybody Loves Raymond*, the dining table and chairs were actually pulled from the set of the award-winning television show—they inspired the pool house's design. Focusing on the functionality of the room, I selected cork floors because they are environmentally friendly and excellent for water absorption. Since the room gets a lot of use from people going inside with wet bathing suits, the upholstered furniture is made out of teakwood and outdoor fabric that is waterproof and doesn't discolor with chlorine.

Bottom: A contemporary carved travertine marble table displaying an Indian goddess sculpture, a 17th-century Italian carving and an early 20th-century sculpture are a harmonious blend of styles and periods. This striking setting was featured in the film *Charlie Wilson's War* and was used in the advertising campaigns of both Versace and Badgley Mischka.

Facing Page Top: An extension of the client's love for the color red, which is predominant inside the home, the 15-foot by 200-foot loggia presents a series of outdoor living and eating areas that harmonize with the sunlight and garden by the addition of yellow and green tones. To ensure ultimate comfort, an indoor chair design was incorporated with outdoor materials such as teakwood and waterproof fabric.

Facing Page Bottom: Directing the tone of the master bedroom was the client's large contemporary art collection. We upholstered the walls in a tan pinstripes outdoor fabric to absorb sound and bring a feeling of coziness to the room; it has the added benefit of protecting against fading from extensive sun exposure and wear-and-tear from children and pets. While a chrome bedside table might have seemed the more obvious choice, an early 19th-century desk gives an unexpected twist to the room. The frame on the large photograph was selected to match the frame depicted in the photo; this provides a fascinating sort of "picture within a picture" effect.
Photographs by Michael McCreary

"People shouldn't have to make a trade off between comfort and beauty. They truly can have both."

—Timothy Corrigan

Specializing in refined, clean-line traditional interior designs, A. LaMar Lisman and his credentialed associates have made their mark in some of the most sophisticated residences throughout Utah and America's western states. The studio's work reflects today's preferred lifestyle of relaxed ease, yet every home possesses a cohesive look that respects tradition with a mix of new elements to make it current. Architectural details, millwork and custom cabinetry, fine furnishings and textiles, unique finishes and exquisite materials selection are expressed in thoughtful ways. LaMar's highly creative approach based on each homeowner's dreams and family requirements has culminated in exquisite residential designs. Inspired by the exciting collaborative process, the talented members of Lisman Studio are poised to restore a splendid period home, oversee a renovation or start with a clean slate in an all-new construction; the grand finale is consistently elegant and inviting.

Spécialisés dans la décoration d'intérieur raffinée, traditionnelle, aux lignes sobres, A. LaMar Lisman et ses associés certifiés ont marqué de leur empreinte certaines des résidences les plus sophistiquées dans tout l'Utah et les états de l'Ouest des États-Unis. Les œuvres du studio sont le reflet du style de vie actuellement privilégié, celui d'une aisance décontractée, mais chacune des maisons présente une apparence cohérente respectueuse de la tradition avec un mélange de nouveaux éléments qui lui donnent un caractère actualisé. Les détails architecturaux, l'ébénisterie et les boiseries sur mesure, les meubles et les textiles, les finitions uniques et le choix de matériaux exquis s'expriment de manière profonde. L'approche hautement créative de LaMar, individualisée en fonction des rêves et des contraintes familiales de chaque propriétaire, aboutit à d'exquises créations résidentielles. Inspirés par le passionnant processus collaboratif, les membres talentueux de Lisman Studio sont prêts à restaurer une splendide résidence d'époque, à superviser une rénovation, ou à faire table rase et entreprendre une construction totalement neuve. Le résultat final est toujours élégant et accueillent.

Especializándose en diseños de interiores refinados, tradicionales y simples, A. LaMar Lisman y sus prestigiosos asociados han dejado su marca en muchas de las residencias más sofisticadas en todo Utah y los estados del oeste de EEUU. La obra del estudio refleja la simplicidad relajada, el estilo de vida preferido de la actualidad, y cada hogar prosee un aspecto cohesivo que respeta lo tradicional con una mezcla de nuevos elementos para un toque de actualidad. Los detalles arquitectónicos, la carpintería y los gabinetes personalizados, mobiliario y textiles de lujo, terminaciones exclusivas y exquisitas selecciones de materiales son expresados de manera muy cuidadosa. El altamente creativo enfoque de LaMar, en base a los sueños y requerimientos de cada propietario, tiene como resultado diseños residenciales exquisitos. Inspirados en un interesante proceso de cooperación, los talentosos miembros de Lisman Studio se encuentran preparados para comenzar la restauración de un esplendido hogar de época, supervisar una remodelación o comenzar de cero con una construcción nueva; el resultado final es consistentemente elegante y atractivo.

A. LaMar Lisman

UTAH

Above Left: Traditional pieces are integrated into a renovated kitchen where Queen Anne style meets modern elements. A contemporary custom display cabinet provides storage and serving options while polished countertops and honed floors of Crema Marfil limestone unify the space.

Above Right: We created a formal living room with two mirror-image fireplace walls for an ethereal atmosphere. Artfully placing the piano lounge and conversational seating, the space is elegantly anchored by a custom-loomed wool carpet with a subtly carved motif.

Facing Page: An English Tudor cottage seamlessly relates to the original manor house with its rich walnut beams, detailed fretwork and mouldings. The bedroom's blend of family heirlooms, an array of glorious fabrics and new Persian rug creates an Old World ambience.

Previous Page: We wanted an established presence for a new home and started with a cream color palette, natural wood and stone elements. The foyer has inlaid travertine and St. Laurent marble; exquisite hand-turned railings and millwork details create a clean, yet traditional look.
Photographs by Scott Zimmerman

"Design should be approachable and improve people's lives."

—LaMar Lisman

Right: Warm hickory flooring leads the way to the new cottage addition; a unique coffered ceiling of dark walnut is lined with imported pressed English paper, bronzed and glazed to resemble finely sculpted plaster.
Photograph by Scott Zimmerman

Facing Page Top: We designed one contemporary showhouse to exhibit a young, modern feeling with fresh contrasts of black and white. Furnishings wear magnified traditional-patterned fabric for a classic look with a chic edge.
Photograph by Darren Goff

Facing Page Bottom: Capturing The Hamptons aesthetic in Utah, our award-winning design features washed coastal colors and an unexpected ladder collection. The pastel custom pillows and striped sisal rug invite relaxation.
Photograph by Scott Zimmerman

For nearly three decades Donna Livingston has worked internationally and throughout the United States, earning a distinguished reputation for creating interior architecture and design of superior quality. The Los Angeles-based firm Donna Livingston Design has developed a signature style over the years, one that considers both interior architecture and furnishings in concert, incorporating high quality and comfort for discerning clientele. More recently, Donna Livingston Design has embarked on creating a custom line of furniture, including elegant dining room chairs and tables in addition to contemporary veneer pieces. The firm's commitment to a hands-on approach and exceeding expectations ensures that design solutions will continue to be of a timeless, refined aesthetic.

Depuis près de trente ans, Donna Livingston travaille dans tous les États-Unis et au niveau international, où elle s'est taillée une réputation de choix en matière de création d'architecture intérieure et de décoration de qualité supérieure. Donna Livingston Design, une société basée à Los Angeles, met depuis des années au point le style caractéristique de sa griffe, qui prend en compte à la fois l'architecture intérieure et l'ameublement, y incorporant une grande qualité et un grand confort à l'intention de sa clientèle avisée. Plus récemment, Donna Livingston Design a entrepris la création d'une ligne personnalisée d'ameublement, en particulier des chaises et tables de salles à manger élégantes, ainsi que de pièces de bois plaqué contemporaines. L'engagement de la société en faveur d'une approche pratique visant à surpasser les attentes permet de faire en sorte que ses créations restent intemporelles, d'une esthétique raffinée.

Durante casi tres décadas, Donna Livingston ha trabajado internacionalmente y a través de EEUU, haciéndose de una reputación distinguida en la creación de arquitectura de interiores y diseño de calidad superior. La compañía Donna Livingston Design, con sede en Los Ángeles, ha desarrollado un estilo característico a través de los años, un estilo que considera en conjunto tanto la arquitectura interior como el mobiliario, incorporando alta calidad y confort para una clientela exigente. Más recientemente Donna Livingston Design se ha dedicado a la creación de una línea personalizada de muebles, incluyendo elegantes sillas y mesas de comedor, además de piezas contemporáneas de enchapado. El compromiso de la compañía a un enfoque práctico y a superar las expectativas garantiza que las soluciones de diseño continuará con una estética atemporal y refinada.

Donna Livingston

CALIFORNIA

Above Left: Warmth abounds in the elegant library thanks to an abundance of mahogany that we bleached for just the right color. We designed all the built-ins and architectural elements; every shelf is lit from above to showcase the books and artifacts.

Above Right: The bathroom included three feet of blank space above the mirror, so I used a beautiful medallion and made it a focal point rather than a large negative space; silk walls and an onyx tub add to the room's elegant splendor.

Facing Page Top: We built the pedestal to showcase the wonderful nude by Aristide Maillol, which is part of the owner's phenomenal art collection. I used the bronze sculpture in the corner to balance the columns, and it is back-lit for added prominence.

Facing Page Bottom: Stunning views toward the Pacific Ocean are the star of the room, but as a whole the space has a quietness and delicate balance ideally suited for respite. The iron and bronze staircase is Venetian plastered underneath and provides a bold architectural element; a Persian rug and chairs upholstered in a Flemish tapestry complete the composition.

Previous Page: I like to start with a strong architectural element, and after taking down a wall dividing two rooms of an Los Angeles penthouse we added antique, gilded Roman columns from the late 18th century. From there we added many layers, such as the recessed gilt ceiling.
Photographs by Durston Saylor

Top: A French rock crystal lamp illuminates the vibrant Chagall painting and the stone box on the desk; the custom-designed desk is a truly extraordinary work of craftsmanship.

Bottom: I designed the walnut bookcases with a thick edge detail, along with down-lighting on all the shelves—almost like rope lighting—to accentuate the homeowner's wonderful rare books and collectibles.

Facing Page Top: Both the bed and desk were custom designed as part of my signature furniture line, and we designed the moulding to wrap around the dramatic bay cove. An aura of warmth and romanticism is balanced by the 10-foot ceiling and dramatic views.

Facing Page Bottom: On a stunning rooftop deck overlooking all of Los Angeles we designed the gazebo, which has automated sunshades that traverse the beams, to define the area. The bronze planters flanking the edge function like a hedge, giving a feeling of infinity—the feeling of a garden on top of the world.
Photographs by Durston Saylor

" I love how every project
is different, every client is
unique, every home is different
architecturally—that's what
makes my job so great."
—Donna Livingston

For Becky Najafi, empty space presents limitless possibilities for creative expression just as a blank canvas does an artist; she believes there is a psychology to every room within a home and collaborates with clients to create sanctuary. A graduate of Arizona State University, Becky began De Atelier Design Group in Scottsdale in 1985 before relocating to Las Vegas in 1989. She loves the diversity of people who live in Las Vegas and the eclectic character they bring to this thriving metropolis—yet remarkable design opportunities take her around the nation and beyond for both commercial and residential endeavors. Becky constantly furthers her education by researching new design techniques, materials and trends, as she believes that is the designer's role to inform the client and present a wide array of opportunities.

Pour Becky Najafi, un espace vide représente des possibilités illimitées d'expression créative tout comme une toile vierge fait un artiste. Elle est convaincue que chaque pièce d'une maison a sa propre psychologie, et collabore avec les clients pour créer leur sanctuaire. Diplômée de l'Arizona State University, Becky a fondé De Atelier Design Group à Scottsdale en 1985 avant de partir pour Las Vegas en 1989. Elle adore la diversité des habitants de Las Vegas et le caractère éclectique qu'ils donnent à cette métropole en pleine expansion. Des opportunités remarquables dans le domaine de l'architecture intérieure la conduisent toutefois dans l'ensemble de la nation et au-delà dans le cadre de projets à la fois commerciaux et résidentiels. Becky ne cesse de se former en recherchant de nouvelles techniques d'architecture, de nouveaux matériaux et de nouvelles tendances, dans la mesure où elle pense que le rôle du designer consiste à informer le client et lui présenter une vaste gamme d'opportunités.

Para Becky Najafi el espacio vacío representa posibilidades ilimitadas para la expresión creativa, de la misma manera que un lienzo lo hace para un artista; considera que existe una psicología para cada habitación dentro de un hogar y colabora con los clientes para crear un santuario. Graduada de la Universidad del Estado de Arizona, Becky creó el De Atelier Design Group en Scottsdale en 1985, antes de mudarse a Las Vegas en 1989. Ama la diversidad de los habitantes de esa ciudad y el carácter ecléctico que aportan a esa vibrante metrópolis, pero sus extraordinarias oportunidades de diseño la llevan por todo el país y el mundo, tanto para proyectos comerciales como residenciales. Becky mejora constantemente su educación mediante la investigación de nuevas técnicas, materiales y tendencias, ya que está convencida de que el rol del diseñador es informar al cliente y presentarle una amplia gama de oportunidades.

Becky Najafi

NEVADA

Above: The music room's warmth and welcoming draw its melodious homeowners back again and again. Art over the piano depicts musical family members while the bamboo reiterates the home's Eastern motif; a gold and bronze mirror and large, carved candlesticks complete the composition.

Right: Covered in multicolored, textured tissue paper, the walls meld copper, red umber and gold overlay with a tactility that begs to be felt. Silk drapes frame the windows and establish engaging proportions; the leather table is flanked by gold leaf chairs adorned with embossed chenille seats.

Facing Page: Thai temple dancers watch over the entry foyer, providing a splash of color in a space that balances formal—exhibited in the immaculate Schonbeck chandelier and stately clock beneath—with an eclectic playfulness. The embossed tapestry chair and wrought iron balustrade are both custom designs.

Previous Page: Again emphasizing the home's Asian theme, the guest master bedroom was inspired by a family kimono. The textured metal light fixture appears as bamboo; it holds a soft light encased in a paper shade. Rich silk drapes cover green wallpaper, which was inspired by the well-traveled homeowners' love of birds. An Asian-styled drum is gold inlaid and completes the prevailing Eastern aura.

Photographs by Studio West Photography

"It is the designer's responsibility to guide clients toward a clear vision for a home of excitement, stimulus, texture and color."

—Becky Najafi

Top: The art-loving homeowners sought a home office that would elegantly coalesce the functional with the aesthetic. Like many of the home's furnishings, I designed the desk to be functional art and had it meticulously crafted by a local artisan. It features a copper front that rises up through the wood surface on the far end.

Bottom: The sink's stone bowl rests atop a unique pedestal, which is designed to light up and create a charming ambience; the mirror further enhances the powder room. The custom terracotta red wall finish and flagstone floor set an engaging tone that is carried throughout the contemporary Southwestern residence.

Facing Page: Large windows bring resplendent Tucson sunsets inside, a phenomenon that is mirrored in the recessed, painted ceiling feature above the alabaster light fixture. I designed the contemporary table base and glass top expressly for the space. The residents' love of purple is on full display; the chairs alternate between crushed chenille and patterned chenille with silk insets for variation. Three sculptural vases were created by artisan David Coddaire.
Photographs by Bill Lesch

The more a person travels from country to country observing the different cultures and design applications, the more he realizes that good design is there to be seen, there to be appreciated and there for expanding one's own boundaries of creativity. Quentin Rance applies this awareness when designing homes around the world. After establishing an enviable career in London, with a large clientele, including quite a few foreign nationals who demanded uniqueness, Quentin moved to Los Angeles, bringing with him the essential international experience that allows his projects to span all styles, with a fresh excitement propelling each undertaking.

Plus on voyage d'un pays à l'autre pour observer des cultures et styles de décoration différents, plus on s'aperçoit que l'on y trouve des créations de qualité, que l'on peut voir, apprécier, et qui permettent d'élargir les limites de la créativité de chacun. Quentin Rance en a conscience lorsqu'il décore des maisons dans le monde entier. Après une carrière enviable à Londres, avec une clientèle importante, dont quelques étrangers à la recherche de créations uniques, Quentin est parti à Los Angeles, équipé de cette expérience internationale essentielle qui permet à ses projets d'englober tous les styles, chaque entreprise lui insufflant une passion renouvelée.

Cuanto más viaja una persona de país en país, observando las diferentes culturas y aplicaciones de diseño, más claro queda que el buen diseño existe para ser visto, apreciado y para expandir los límites de la creatividad. Quentin Rance aplica ese principio al diseño de hogares en todo el mundo. Después de una envidiable carrera en Londres, con una amplia clientela, entre los que se encuentran numerosos extranjeros con exigencias de exclusividad, Quentin se mudó a Los Ángeles, llevando consigo la experiencia internacional esencial que permite que sus proyectos alcancen todos los estilos con un entusiasmo fresco que impulsa cada nuevo compromiso.

Quentin Rance

"Good design is international."

—Quentin Rance

Above: The Bel Air home—a California Ranch-style home—was one of the most unique projects I've ever done. The Gene Autry Museum was the perfect research facility to capture the Native American aesthetic. The central adobe fireplace is double sided, which controls flow and allows fragmenting for the surround spaces. The remarkable Indian head painting is by Kevin Redstar.

Facing Page Top: The design is such that you can never be in anyone's way. Soft wall colors allow the furniture and artwork to stand out. The continuity of the color scheme is effective.

Facing Page Bottom: Comfortable seating surrounds the space and features the fine oil painting *Blessings from Above* by George Hallmark.

Previous Page: The entrance with the rotunda ceiling has arched recesses to display the unusual bronze entitled *Thunderbird* by Tammy Garcia and a marvelous carved and textured marble Indian figure by Oreland Joe. Lighting for the artwork throughout the home was carefully evaluated and installed to enhance the homeowner's outstanding Southwestern art collection.
Photographs by Peter Christiansen Valli

"To achieve the perfect design idea, you must do thorough research and have infinite patience."

—Quentin Rance

Top: The carved marble Indian couple is an exceptionally detailed piece by Oreland Joe.

Center: We used stronger colors from the Southwestern color palette to make the formal dining room dramatic.

Bottom: John Coleman's striking bronze statue, *The Guardian*, is a perfect entry piece for the home.

Facing Page Top: The hutch in the breakfast room is great for displaying smaller pieces of Southwestern art, one of which is the fascinating Rose Pecos piece called *Indian Storyteller*.

Facing Page Bottom: The area completes the walkable circle around the central fireplace and looks out to the pool and the landscaped garden.
Photographs by Peter Christiansen Valli

For more than a decade Garret Cord Werner has been creating stunning interior spaces. Whether residential or public, the interiors achieve functionality and understated elegance, as Garret approaches each design through a sophisticated lens of fine architectural detail and dynamic spatial awareness. This approach expands the firm's artistic scope beyond furniture and ornamentation to provide a strong sense of harmony in every space. Garret and his team fuse metropolitan necessities such as storage, convenience, and multiuse spaces with elements of technology, color, light and shape to compose beautiful and award-winning interiors.

Depuis plus de dix ans, Garret Cord Werner crée des espaces intérieurs éblouissants. Qu'il s'agisse d'intérieurs résidentiels ou publics, ses œuvres sont caractérisées par leur fonctionnalité et leur élégance discrète, dans la mesure où Garret aborde chaque création sous l'angle sophistiqué des détails architecturaux et d'une conscience spatiale dynamique. Cette approche élargit la portée artistique des travaux de la société au-delà les meubles et de l'ornementation, et lui permet d'infuser un sens de l'harmonie à chaque espace. Garret et son équipe réalisent la fusion de nécessités métropolitaines telles le rangement, la commodité et des espaces polyvalents avec des éléments de technologie, couleur, lumière et espace qui permettent de composer de magnifiques intérieurs primés.

Durante más de una década, Garret Cord Werner ha creado magníficos espacios interiores. Los espacios, residenciales o públicos, logran funcionalidad y una sutil elegancia, ya que Garret encara cada diseño a través del sofisticado lente del detalle arquitectónico minucioso y una conciencia espacial dinámica. Dicho enfoque expande el alcance artístico de la compañía más allá de los muebles y lo ornamental para brindar un sólido sentido de armonía en cada espacio. Garret y su equipo fusionan las necesidades metropolitanas, tales como el almacenamiento y los espacios de usos múltiples, con los elementos de tecnología, color, luz y forma para componer bellos y distinguidos interiores.

Garret Cord Werner

WASHINGTON

Above: Strong spatial geometry and balance, reinforced by natural lighting, appear in the dramatic contemporary bathroom. A raised platform for the sculptural bath defines the area, while the wood floor serves to catch overflowing water in the Japanese soaking environment. Both bathtub and sink are made of stone slab, harmonizing the room through understated repetition.
Rendering by Garret Cord Werner, LLC

Right: Simple and pure materials, natural colors and refined details in an area with one strong artistic element can make for a strong lasting impression. The dramatic sculpture is a carved African Robed Wanderer, a sign of welcome and greetings.
Photograph by Benjamin Benschneider

Facing Page Top & Bottom: A strong architectural approach to the interior is reinforced with built-in storage and display areas. Successfully blending form with function became crucial; organic materials and textures offer a tranquil feeling while providing everyday necessities. One entity, encompassing interest and diversity, results from blending various materials with common palettes.
Photographs by Roger Davies

Previous Page: As the most eye-catching element in the room, the shower has more of a purpose than simple aesthetics. It serves as a lens to the stone vanity, almost magnifying the natural ambience. The raised floor makes plumbing changes accessible and defines the area without adding walls. Stone surfaces add texture and organic quality to the interior while reinforcing the vision of exterior space. Lighting, including floor-mounted custom lamps and in-floor landscape lighting, enhances the outdoor concept.
Photograph by Alex Hayden

"An outside-in philosophy, harmonizing the exterior architecture and interior design of a building allows our design to become greater than its sum, an integral part of the whole rather than superfluous elements within."

—Garret Cord Werner

Top & Bottom: Our highly detailed bed and bathing suites have won regional and national recognition over the years. Custom bedroom furnishings and linens are possible for residents who are looking to individualize their dwellings. A personally tailored area takes on the personality of the homeowners; a vanity sink with a pedestal base and floor-mounted spout create an understated, peaceful space.

Facing Page: Urban elegance can be both casual and stunning, as long as dynamic spatial awareness is maintained—a reoccurring philosophy in all of our work. This break from a more conventional approach expands the artistic scope and results in a strong sense of harmony. Simultaneously romantic, sophisticated and laid-back, the room's space is carefully occupied by soft drapery and a floating bath: Nothing is haphazard.
Photographs by Steve Keating

A talented and diverse group of experienced design professionals, Scottsdale-based Wiseman & Gale Interiors has been creating luxurious, Southwest-inspired interiors for more than four decades. The firm's 10 designers are led by the gifted quartet of Sue Calvin, Jana Parker Lee, Patty Burdick and her son, Scott Burdick. Wiseman & Gale is known for working very closely with clients to ensure that the design process is fun yet thorough, allowing for a creative and interactive relationship to develop. Additionally, Wiseman & Gale's designers are helped by their world-class showroom, featuring antiques and accessories sourced from around the world, hand-selected to complement the firm's one-of-a-kind designs. It is no wonder that Wiseman & Gale has established itself as the premier residential interior design firm in the Southwest.

Wiseman & Gale Interiors, dont le siège se trouve à Scottsdale, est un groupe talentueux et diversifié de professionnels expérimentés du domaine de l'architecture, et crée des intérieurs luxueux s'inspirant de l'esthétique du Sud-Ouest depuis plus de quarante ans. Les 10 designers de l'entreprise travaillent sous la direction d'un groupe débordant de talent constitué par Sue Calvin, Jana Parker Lee, Patty Burdick et son fils Scott Burdick. Wiseman & Gale est réputée pour son travail en très étroite collaboration avec ses clients pour faire en sorte que chaque processus de conception reste constamment divertissant, et permette l'instauration d'une relation créative et interactive. Les designers de Wiseman & Gale disposent également d'un salon d'exposition de classe mondiale, présentant des meubles antiques et des accessoires en provenance du monde entier, choisis avec soin pour compléter les conceptions uniques de la société. Il n'est donc pas surprenant que Wiseman & Gale se soit imposé comme le premier cabinet d'architecture intérieure résidentielle du Sud-Ouest.

Wiseman & Gale Interiors, un talentoso y diverso grupo de experimentados profesionales del diseño con sede en Scottsdale, ha creado lujosos interiores inspirados en el Sudoeste de EEUU por más de cuatro décadas. Los 10 diseñadores de la compañía están liderados por el talentoso cuarteto de Sue Calvin, Jana Parker Lee, Patty Burdick y su hijo Scott Burdick. Wiseman & Gale es famoso por trabajar en estrecha colaboración con los clientes para asegurarse de que el proceso de diseño resulte al mismo tiempo divertido y minucioso, haciendo posible el desarrollo de una relación creativa e interactiva. Adicionalmente, los diseñadores de Wiseman & Gale reciben la contribución de su sala de exposición de nivel internacional, que incluye antigüedades y accesorios de todo el mundo, seleccionados cuidadosamente para complementar los diseños exclusivos de la compañía. No es para sorprenderse de que Wiseman & Gale se haya establecido como la principal compañía de diseño de interiores residencial del Sudoeste de EEUU.

Wiseman & Gale

ARIZONA